the Mindful Garden

the *the* Mindful Garden

serene spaces for outdoor living

STEPHANIE DONALDSON
with photography by MELANIE ECLARE

RYLAND PETERS & SMALL
LONDON • NEW YORK

For Ben

Design Megan Smith and Emily Breen
Senior editor Clare Double
Picture research Emily Westlake
   and Jess Walton
Production manager
   Gordana Simakovic
Creative director Leslie Harrington
Publishing director Alison Starling

First published in 2003. This revised
edition published in 2024 by
Ryland Peters & Small
20–21 Jockey's Fields
London WC1R 4BW
and
341 East 116th Street
New York, NY 10029
www.rylandpeters.com

10 9 8 7 6 5 4 3 2 1

Text © 2003, 2024 Stephanie Donaldson
Design © 2024 Ryland Peters & Small
Photography © 2003, 2024 Ryland
Peters & Small, except the following
photographs © Steve Painter: 104l, 105r

ISBN 978 1 78879 595 1

A CIP record for this book is available
from the British Library

Printed and bound in China

Front cover: Dan Duchars/The garden
of Nyla Abraham and Paul Sadler of
@_thesuburbancottagegarden_ in Bath.
Back cover: Melanie Eclare/The garden
and nursery De Brinkhof of Riet Brinkhof
and Joop Van Den Berk.
Spine: Andrea Jones.

MIX
Paper from
responsible sources
FSC® C106563

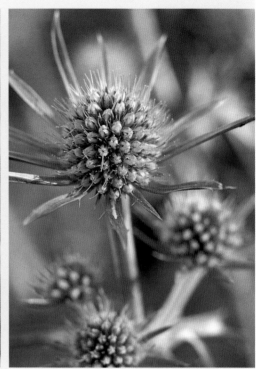

Contents

Introduction

We live in a stressful world where we all need a haven, a place to forget our usual concerns – somewhere we can be simple, re-establish our place in the natural order of things and experience contentment, even if it is only for a few moments. There are people who lose themselves in books, others find physical exercise is the key, but for true mindfulness there is little to rival time spent in a garden. The fears and frustrations of life soon recede when there is direct contact with nature.

How you choose to spend your time in the garden is very much a matter of personal preference. It may be that you are never happier than when you are trundling along behind your lawnmower, while someone else may choose to lie in a hammock and gaze at the sky through a canopy of leaves and others will find true contentment by growing their own vegetables. Your choice will inevitably dictate your garden's appearance, but before making any changes it is always wise to separate the realizable dreams from the fantasies. The potager at Villandry is a glory to behold, but it is also extremely work intensive and

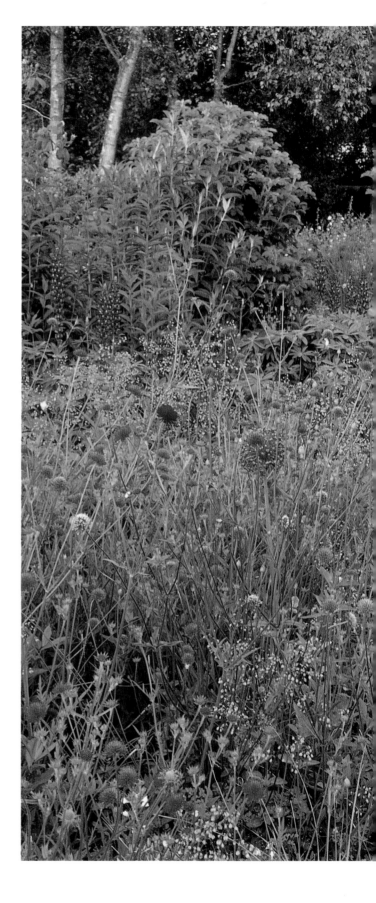

RIGHT An apparently carefree, informal garden demands a gardener who is happy with a degree of untidiness. To keep it in flower throughout the growing season is an endless task – far better to accept that it has its high spots and sit back and relax at other times, leaving the plants to set seed and ensure continuity in the years ahead. This style of garden is for those who work with nature rather than those who seek to control it.

the opportunities to take your ease in a garden of this kind are few and far between. However, a modest vegetable plot tucked behind a picket fence can be decorative, productive and a peaceful place. Consider carefully before you embark on creating your dream garden – small changes can be as effective as grand designs.

A mindful garden – simple or harmonious to look at, restful to sit in – is a place of balance, sufficiently demanding of your time to be satisfying without enslaving you. It's the place where you can be your true self, relaxed and at ease – a place where you feel free to be sad, happy or even a little sentimental. In the mindful garden listening to the song of a bird or smelling a rose are as important as weeding; they should touch all the senses and leave you feeling enriched. In the most literal way, you can 'earth' yourself by putting your hands in the soil. So many of life's experiences today are indirect – our food often comes from the other side of the planet, the music we listen to is recorded, we communicate via mobile phone or the internet – so when we cultivate the soil and plant a seed or seedling, nurture it and watch it grow, the wonder and satisfaction we feel are very precious.

LEFT Classic Adirondack chairs, painted white to contrast with the green foliage, surround a small firepit in this inviting outdoor room. The lilac tree provides uplifting colour and fragrance in the springtime.

Peaceful
Shapes AND
SPACES

'Peace' is a word that engages heart and head – we feel it with our emotions as we understand it with our intellect. This is a central element in the creation of a successful mindful garden. When considering any aspect of the design, check your emotional response to your plans as well as practical aspects. Remember that you are seeking a calming rather than a stimulating effect.

RIGHT The curving slate wall defines and separates the different areas in this garden designed by Roberto Silva. At the far end, wooden decking creates a spacious outdoor room simply furnished with a table and chairs.

Keeping it simple

Simplicity is key. Often the starting point is what is removed rather than what is added. Taking away fussy detail and clutter and restricting the colour palette has an immediate calming effect that is both visually and emotionally satisfying. This is true of the planting as well as the solid elements contained within the garden.

A garden is not just what happens within its boundaries – it is also profoundly influenced by its surroundings. Understanding these additional influences will help you create the mindful, calming retreat you desire.

Where a garden is bordered by open countryside, distant views, other mature gardens or parkland, it should take advantage of what is known by designers as the 'borrowed view'. Allow the space to flow into its surroundings, using the landscape to lift and lead the eye to the wider view. Conversely, if buildings or unattractive features are visible from the garden, or it is enclosed by trees with no view beyond, concentrate on the inner view. Keep focal points at low levels so that the eye is engaged by what is within the

PREVIOUS PAGE LEFT Wide, shallow steps – the treads and margins softened by plants – lead to a mown path that curves away into the distance. Matching the width of the path and steps creates a broad avenue for a companionable stroll.

PREVIOUS PAGE RIGHT A path mown through a meadow brings you close to the beauty of the grasses without the need to trample them underfoot. The play of light on the grass creates an ever-changing mood.

ABOVE Concealing the labour-intensive kitchen garden behind a woven fence allows the gardener to sit and enjoy the view without being lured away from a quiet, restful moment by any task that needs doing.

garden's boundaries and does not look upwards and outwards. In either case, the eye should travel smoothly across what it sees rather than jumping from spot to spot.

When making use of the wider view, remember that it will be most effective if you resist making the garden itself too busy. Large areas of grass, some mown, some left to grow long, with a few carefully positioned trees, will lead seamlessly to the view beyond. It is no accident that in many historic gardens, the herbaceous borders and potagers are contained within walls or hedges. Their impact is all the greater when confined, and so positioned they do not detract from the surrounding landscape. In a small garden which benefits from a good view, a similar effect can be achieved by restricting borders and structures to the area closest to the house, gradually paring down the planting and hard landscaping so that at the end of the space, adjacent to the view, the garden is at its simplest and least contrived.

Unlike the owners of the great gardens, most people who live in the country do not have a belt of parkland separating them from the more industrial aspects of agriculture – fields left uncultivated, muddy pastures or functional farm buildings – so it is generally advisable to have an informal boundary between the garden and the fields beyond. A mixed hedge of indigenous shrubs and trees works well – especially if one or two trees are allowed to grow tall and frame the view. Selective pruning of this type of boundary can work wonders (left untrimmed it is a barrier); cut lower in places to open up a view or echo the curves of the landscape beyond, it becomes part of the bigger picture.

Where a fence is necessary it is best kept low, rustic in appearance and preferably open, for example using a post and rail design. This type of fence can always be made animal- or childproof by attaching wire netting, while still retaining the view beyond.

Where good views are absent, the mindful garden needs to exclude the world beyond its boundaries. It is a more intimate and enclosed space and sometimes consists of little more than a tabletop display, a balcony or a courtyard.

OPPOSITE A shallow bowl emulates the arid landscape where these succulents would grow naturally. The pebbles prevent soil splashing onto the leaves during watering.

ABOVE The tiniest windowsill, balcony or terrace can contain miniature landscapes of great subtlety. Here, a leaf-shaped carved rock emerges from a bed of gravel. Carefully placed succulents complete the picture.

RIGHT The uncluttered simplicity of this courtyard is reminiscent of a Japanese temple or a monastic cloister. The grass growing in the central stone block is the only touch of green.

In less rural surroundings privacy becomes a major consideration. However fabulous the borrowed view, if it opens the garden to passers-by or neighbours, some screening will be necessary or its peacefulness will be compromised. A fence topped by trellis through which plants can twine both conceals and reveals the view beyond. A tall hedge neatly trimmed into undulating curves rather than a horizontal line can be used to frame the best of the view while masking most of the garden from the outside. Seasonal screening in the shape of deciduous trees, shrubs and climbers ensures privacy in the summer months when the garden is most used, yet opens up views during the rest of the year. This type of

garden can be both inward and outward looking, depending on the season.

In urban or other situations where good views are absent, the mindful garden needs to exclude the world beyond its boundaries. It is a more intimate and enclosed space and sometimes consists of little more than a carefully arranged tabletop display, a balcony or a courtyard. Here in particular, it is the atmosphere rather than the dimensions of the garden which creates the mood. Although a barrier of trees and shrubs seems the obvious way to separate the garden from its surroundings, this can sometimes prove problematic in an urban environment. If you are overlooked by tall buildings and buffeted by gusts of wind, it may prove difficult to establish the plants, and where they do grow successfully, the result can be a dank, damp and shady garden with sour soil. In this situation the hard landscaping needs to be strong and well thought out, creating focal points and harmonious shapes that draw the eye so that the planting becomes less central. A few carefully chosen architectural plants will have far more impact and be easier to take care of than a motley selection of undemanding shrubs that is tolerant of urban conditions.

It is particularly important to relate form to function in the urban garden. However beautifully designed a garden is, if it can't be used in the way its owner envisaged, it

OPPOSITE A rooftop terrace is sheltered from the wind and hidden from a nearby block of flats by large-scale but simple planting that is in perfect harmony with the minimalist architecture and furniture.

ABOVE An urban garden keeps planting to a minimum and relies on sculptural shapes and dramatic lighting for impact – this is somewhere to look at rather than a place in which to relax. Although low maintenance, this type of garden needs regular attention to ensure the gravel stays free of fallen leaves and weeds, or it quickly looks neglected.

RIGHT Careful pruning has revealed the sculptural shape of the tree that shades this city garden. Rather than attempting to grow other plants, which would dilute its impact and possibly struggle to survive in its shade, the designer Jonathan Bell has created textured horizontal surfaces on two levels. A simple trellis fence encloses the garden, giving it some privacy without depriving it of borrowed light. A vase of sunflowers adds a temporary splash of colour.

cannot be considered a success. The conflicting emotions that result will be far from peaceful. It is important to ask yourself how you plan to make use of your garden before embarking on any changes, and any good garden designer will ask you detailed questions about what you want from your garden before redesigning it.

Different people want different things. Some city dwellers want nothing more than a beautiful, undemanding space to look out on. They have neither the time nor the inclination to garden. They simply want somewhere that is soothing to look at at the end of a stressful day. This minimalist style of garden is very much the province of childless urbanites. A family would find that it caused more conflict than harmony when children scattered such a garden with toys or grazed their knees on raked gravel surfaces, and a keen gardener would soon grow frustrated by the lack of plants. While most people will fill a balcony or terrace with plants, others see it as an outdoor room that needs nothing more than a few carefully chosen pieces of furniture. It may irritate friends and family who long to decorate the space with plants, but if a sparsely furnished outdoor room is your idea of a mindful garden, outsiders should not be allowed to interfere.

These days, when many of us work from home, our gardens have a new role. Any part of the garden that leads from a work space needs to be restful to look at, but not necessarily inviting or it will prove a distraction. In my own case, the view from my desk is of treetops and sky – good

for gazing at while I think, but not directly engaging. Initially I had planned to put my desk in another room where there is a view of the sea, but I realized that I would never get any work done. The ever-changing moods of the sea and the comings and goings of the fishing boats would have proved far more interesting than the task in hand. For work spaces in particular, keep the outlook simple. Avoid fussy details or planting – a single well-

tended plant or tree is more appropriate than a border full of flowers that will lure you out to dead-head or prune.

When it comes to planting, simplicity and restraint are more calming than busy borders incorporating single specimens of numerous varieties of plant. If you are a plant enthusiast it is easy to get carried away and end up with something that is more plant zoo than garden as you strive to include every plant that takes your fancy. When making a mindful garden it is necessary to temper this tendency and adopt a 'less is more' approach. This is true of colour too – the use of a limited palette is more soothing to the eye than a vibrant mixture which can easily be overstimulating and is definitely not tranquil in its effect. Avoid combining colours which intensify one another and choose instead those that blend subtly together. Anyone familiar with the English countryside will

ABOVE Folding chairs and a couple of rustic tables beckon invitingly, the perfect setting for a summer meal in the garden. It's tempting to imagine that the tethered goats are four-legged lawnmowers, but as they are more browsers than grazers they will probably be more interested in the food on the table.

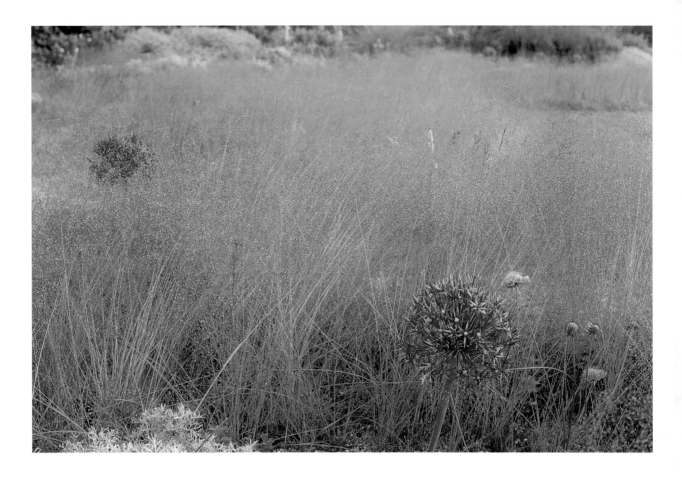

know that the different shades and shapes of green that make up its meadows and woodlands create a supremely beautiful and peaceful environment. On a smaller scale this use of subtle shades rather than contrasting colours can have the same effect.

In a rural garden, using improved cultivars of the wild flowers that grow locally, in natural-looking drifts, will create a seamless blend with the countryside beyond. Cultivars select the best qualities of the wild flower but frequently have larger blooms and longer flowering periods. Be cautious in your use of true wild flowers unless they are from an assured source; plundering the local flora is not recommended.

In a garden with large areas of lawn, a mown path can be very appealing as it curves sinuously through the long grass. The sight of long grass rippling in the wind has a quiet beauty that rivals the colourful displays of flowers in many cultivated gardens.

Leaf shape and plant outline are elements which should be considered when planning a garden. This doesn't necessarily mean that you should always seek out plants with rounded leaves and gentle curves, but that the plants you choose should enhance the atmosphere of the garden. In a minimalist garden a plant with striking, architectural foliage is more appropriate than a rose – however beautiful the rose may be, it will look out of place and feel discordant in such a setting.

OPPOSITE Planting that echoes the local flora can link a country garden to the landscape. Here, swathes of *Geranium phaeum* fill the foreground and pathways zigzag towards the arching branches of a *Buddleja alternifolia*.

ABOVE Inspired planting at Sticky Wicket, created by Peter and Pam Lewis. The russety-pink haze of flowering cloud grass is punctuated by *Allium cristophii* and pink scabious. The dried seedheads will add interest later in the year.

RIGHT By limiting the palette of colours you use in a garden, you can calm the effect of a complex planting scheme. The various shapes, shades and textures in this formal front garden create a pleasing green tapestry. Slight touches of other colours highlight the general theme. Colour-themed gardens are always most effective when other colours make subtle appearances, otherwise the effect can be dull.

Water is a wonderful addition. Keep the garden tranquil with rills that flow imperceptibly or still pools that reflect their surroundings. Choose simple shapes – rectangles, squares or circles.

These days it seems that no garden is complete unless it has a water feature of some sort or another, and there is no doubt that, used correctly, water is a wonderful addition to a mindful garden. A gently bubbling fountain becomes a focal point and you will become lost in a world of your own as you listen to its soothing sound and watch the movement of the water. Remember however that fast-moving water has an energizing effect, which may disrupt the contemplative mood. Avoid anything that splashes noisily or flows at a hectic pace – keep the garden tranquil with rills that flow imperceptibly or still pools that reflect their surroundings. Choose simple shapes – rectangles, squares or circles rather than peculiar amorphous outlines.

Don't forget the practicalities either. When installing water features in a garden it is always advisable to consult an expert – few things can spoil the mood of a space more effectively than a poorly installed pond that turns a murky green at the drop of a hat and requires endless maintenance. If the complexities of pumps and filters, wiring and water supplies all prove too expensive and time-consuming, you can simply grow waterlilies in large, water-filled, glazed pots. Waterlilies love deep, still water and will grow happily this way, especially if they are in partial shade. Choose a slow-growing or miniature variety to suit your container or alternatively divide the plant every other year.

Small or large, inward or outward looking, every garden needs somewhere to sit. Bear in mind that the style of seating and the materials used for the hard landscaping should relate to the rest of the garden. Concrete paving slabs look fine in a contemporary urban garden, and

ABOVE A rill flows across a roof terrace in a shallow galvanized trough. Stones in the water echo the pebbles around it and a willow casts dappled shade.

OPPOSITE Still water acts as a mirror, reflecting the surrounding trees and the sky above. Try to avoid overhanging branches, or your pool will be filled with brown leaves in the autumn.

decking is entirely appropriate in a waterside site, but used elsewhere these surfaces can look uncomfortably out of place in their surroundings. When peacefulness is the aim these dissonant associations should be avoided. Seating, too, should be chosen with care – but in choosing a suitable style don't get so carried away by the aesthetic that you end up with something that is wonderful to look at but impossibly uncomfortable. Remember form and function – and simplicity.

Symmetry and balance

Consider the difference between symmetry and balance within the mindful garden. Symmetry mirrors one side of the garden with the other, while balance combines differing features in a pleasing way. Symmetry is a matter of precision and can be achieved intellectually, whereas balance requires feeling.

Most people have a preference for either symmetry or balance. Symmetry is more ordered and predictable, while balance can be fluid or curvaceous. If you are uncertain which you prefer to be guided by, the photographs in this book may help you decide – do you instinctively favour formal regularity, or does a more free-form garden appeal to you?

It is also important to take the shape of your garden into consideration. The space must sit comfortably within its boundaries. It is much trickier to achieve symmetry in an area which is asymmetrical in shape than in a neatly rectangular garden, and it is equally difficult to ignore the influence of the geometry on this shape of garden if you have something less formal in mind. Either way, bear in mind that your intuition is often the best

guide, and it is only when something clearly isn't working that this type of analysis comes in useful.

The founding principle of a symmetrical garden is mirroring. Angles match, paths are central or flanking the centre and except for when a large object creates a focal point at the end of a vista, ornamentation is used in pairs.

ABOVE Pairs of box cones contribute to the symmetry of this formal garden. They also help lift the eye from the strong horizontals of the pond, the paving and the clipped hedges.

OPPOSITE The dark surface of the pond reflects light from the sky above and creating new perspectives. Almost lost in front of the sago palm in its green planter, the flowering spike of the acanthus gains definition in the reflection.

When it works, symmetry is emotionally and visually satisfying, but when it isn't quite right, the result can induce anxiety rather than calm – something to be avoided in a mindful garden.

Planning helps; with the aid of a ruler and a set square (or garden design software), drawing a symmetrical garden on paper is not difficult. Even if you have never done this type of thing before you will quickly see if the proposed shapes sit well with one another. Doing this also reveals

an intriguing aspect of the symmetrical garden. While it should be divided into two even halves across its width, if the same is done lengthways the proportions seldom work, nor if it is divided into quarters. If necessary, it should be divided into thirds.

It is important that paths within the garden have a destination. This may sound obvious, but it is not unusual to visit gardens where a path does nothing more than lead from the house to the fence at the end of the property.

A beautifully planted pot, a seat facing a view, a statue or a water feature all have the power to lure you to the furthest end of the garden.

It may have access points to different parts of the garden along its way, but the lack of an arrival point can be disappointing. This is readily remedied by placing an object at the end of the path – a focal point, either modest or grand – which will draw you towards it. A beautifully planted pot, a seat facing a wonderful view, a statue or a water feature all have the power to lure you to the furthest end of the garden.

Perspective is an important element in this type of garden and there are tricks that can emphasize this effect and make a space seem larger than it actually is. A central path that tapers as it recedes towards the end of the garden will mislead the eye into thinking that the plot is longer than it is in reality, an effect that can be enhanced by gradually reducing the size of any pots flanking the path.

Topiary is very much at home in the formal garden – it helps emphasize symmetry far more effectively than less structured plants. Where space is restricted, topiary looks best when it is limited to no more than two different shapes, and it should always be placed in mirrored pairs or it will unsettle the atmosphere. In a large garden you have more freedom – if the layout is symmetrical, some variation in topiary shapes can introduce a lighter mood.

Not everyone responds positively to the formal rigidity of a symmetrical garden

OPPOSITE The formality of the clipped bay trees presents a contrast to the rustic fencing and kitchen-garden planting of the potager beyond. The trees are evidence that although the potager may be less formal, it will still be orderly.

ABOVE The geometry created by the three stone balls in this Irish garden is gloriously undermined by the untrimmed nature of the copper beech hedge, resulting in a pleasing balance of formality and informality.

If your mindful garden is a place of balance, gentle curves define shape and contemporary materials challenge the old order, creating something new, yet still evoking a sense of restfulness.

though, even if it is softened by planting. If it all seems too contrived and ordered for your taste, you may feel more at home if your mindful garden is a place of balance rather than symmetry. Here gentle curves define shape and contemporary materials challenge the old order, creating something new, yet still evoking a sense of restfulness.

Although there are exceptions, the balanced garden is generally less structured than its symmetrical counterpart, with its architectural elements placed among informal planting. There are fewer obvious guidelines than in the symmetrical garden and consequently much more experimentation is called for. This approach is not suitable for anyone who is likely to fret when confronted by uncertainty. The aim is to create a peaceful garden, but if you have sleepless nights as your garden evolves it becomes rather self-defeating.

If however you are attracted by this style of garden you may find that it is more difficult to visualize on paper than is a geometric design. Curves are better marked out on the ground, and when it comes to placing objects in the

OPPOSITE Pairs of terracotta pots planted with white daisies stand on plinths along a central path. Surrounded by clipped box hedging, the pots draw the eye to the ultimate destination – the pretty white-painted bench at the end of the path.

ABOVE Flanked by box balls, an antique bench is given added importance. Painted a strong shade of blue, its delicate tracery pattern stands out against the foliage and echoes the colour of the paving.

RIGHT There is a pleasing symmetry to this tableau. A clipped tree stands like a green parasol over a pair of painted wooden chairs and terracotta pots planted with box balls.

You may you may know nothing about garden design, but have a strong, instinctive feeling for colours and shapes that combine harmoniously - creating a garden in this way can be a delightfully liberating affair.

garden it is best to experiment with different spots until they feel right. If the object itself is too large, heavy or tall to move easily from place to place, try replacing it with something more manageable that is approximately the same shape and size. You can do an awful lot with a few canes and a ball of string, a chair or a stepladder and some imagination. Half-close your eyes and check the effect of the positioning on the rest of the garden – and remember to check how you feel about what you see as well as what you think. Too often we discount intuition, but it is a very useful tool.

When we look at a work of art and feel uplifted and enriched by it, we don't necessarily understand the principles of proportion or perspective or have a grasp of colour theory, but we often have a positive emotional response that is just as valid as a more informed analysis of the canvas. Similarly, you may know nothing about garden design, but have a strong, instinctive feeling for colours and shapes that combine harmoniously – creating a garden in this way can be a delightfully liberating affair. Free of the constraints of rules and fashion, you can shape a garden that is truly yours.

OPPOSITE A curving path leads sinuously towards a half-concealed tower at the end of the garden. Low-growing bamboo lines the left-hand side of the path, while on the other side a line of large stones draws the eye to your destination.

ABOVE There is a satisfying balance to the curve of this informal hedge, which is echoed by the gravel path and the clean-cut edge where it borders the lawn.

ABOVE At Sticky Wicket in Dorset a precise geometry of radiating circles underlies the Impressionistic planting. To achieve such a natural-looking result requires real plant knowledge and careful management, or it could end up looking like a once-formal garden now overtaken by weeds. At the heart of the garden is a circular chamomile lawn.

LEFT This monolithic, minimalist-style garden is not for the faint-hearted or for those who have a penchant for soft planting, but it undoubtedly has an austere beauty. Over the wall a tree attempts to break in, but within its boundaries only a small square of grass relieves a courtyard that is more about architecture than horticulture.

How you achieve balance is a matter of personal judgement. If you feel happy in your garden and there is nothing you want to change, then trust that feeling. You already have your mindful space, regardless of the dictates of fashion or the opinions of others.

This is not to suggest that balance is unconstrained – far from it, think of traditional scales where all the weight starts off on one side – but the constraints are of your own devising, rather than externally imposed, and how you achieve the balance you seek is a matter of personal judgement. If this all sounds rather esoteric, it isn't. If you feel happy in your garden and there is nothing you want to change, then trust that feeling. You already have your mindful space, regardless of the dictates of fashion or the opinions of others.

Whether your goal is a garden of balance or symmetry, you should consider its relationship with the architecture of your home and its surroundings. You may have your heart set on a wildflower garden with untrimmed mixed hedging, long grass and no visibly cultivated areas, but if the setting is a suburban street it may look more neglected than wild, causing resentment among your neighbours – and your mindful garden will become a bone of contention rather than a place of sanctuary as intended. Similarly, a modernist house needs a garden that is sympathetic to its architecture, rather than a recreation of some earlier gardening style, or the two will rub up against one another in an uncomfortable manner. The wider view is always an important consideration.

RIGHT Clipped squares of box give this rural garden designed by Tania Compton a formal symmetry that is made more relaxed by their planting with a mixture of roses and herbaceous perennials. In the summer flowers spill over the hedges, disguising the underlying geometry that is more evident during the winter months.

Contemplation and relaxation

As you plan your mindful garden it is important to remember that it is as much about how the garden is used as about how it looks – a balancing of form and function. Ideally it should be multifunctional, with open areas for family activities and entertaining as well as quiet places and hidden corners that are conducive to private contemplation.

The moods conjured up by the words contemplation and relaxation are quite different. There is a weight and seriousness, sometimes even a spiritual dimension to contemplation, which is generally thought of as a solitary activity, while relaxation is more about physical repose or socializing. To accommodate both within the same garden requires an awareness of these differences.

There is a long history of great or profound thoughts taking place in a garden, from the dawning self-awareness of Adam and Eve as they contemplated their nakedness in the Garden of Eden to Isaac Newton's formulation of the theory of gravity after he was struck on the head by a falling apple. While most of us are unlikely to change the course of history or increase scientific knowledge when we are lost in thought in the garden, we can take inspiration from historical gardens and incorporate into our own some of the elements that have long been believed to aid contemplation.

RIGHT The curve of this hammock perfectly echoes the contour of the arch above it, but the unforgiving stone beneath is not ideal. It may be better to hang a hammock above grass or some other soft surface.

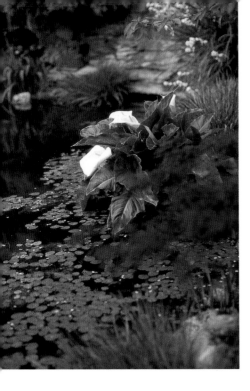

OPPOSITE **A wooden jetty like this one allows close examination of a pond and its teeming life. Both practical and pleasurable, it makes the pond easier to look after and more accessible for enjoyment. Simply remove your shoes and sit on its edge dabbling your feet in the water to experience a perfect moment of relaxation.**

LEFT **Water is the great life-giver, and contemplating it is both thought-provoking and relaxing. A wildlife pond is beneficial for you and the environment alike.**

BELOW **With the addition of a chair, this classical portico by a formal pond would be a perfect place to read a Jane Austen novel and dream of Mr Darcy.**

Zen, ancient Persian and monastic gardens all explored the meaning of life in different ways. Zen emphasizes contemplation and meditation as ways to achieve self-knowledge, and its highly symbolic gardens represent the pathway to enlightenment. The symmetry, order and symbolism of a traditional Persian garden are an earthly representation of paradise. The very word has its origins in Old Persian, in which *pardeiza* meant an enclosed area.

Water was the central, essential element in these gardens; it ensured fertility and cooled the air, but above all it was a metaphor for looking into the soul – as the pools of water mirrored one's image, so the garden was a place for spiritual reflection. During the Middle Ages the cloister gardens of the monastic orders were generally unadorned areas of grass, free from distraction for those who moved in prayer around their perimeters. The physic or infirmary gardens, in which the monks grew

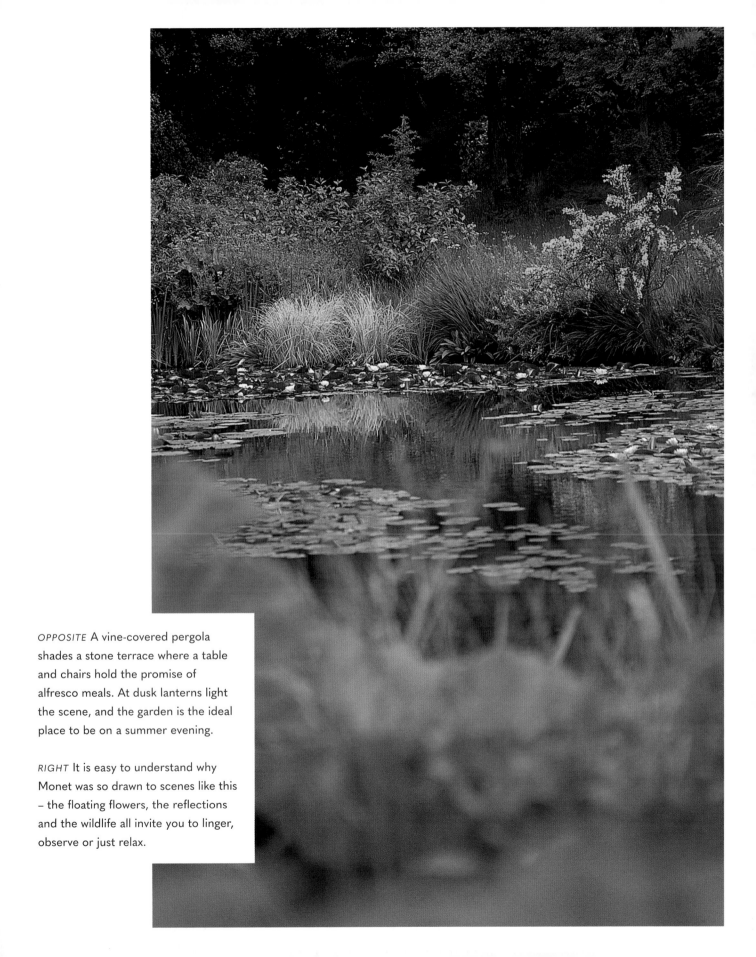

OPPOSITE A vine-covered pergola shades a stone terrace where a table and chairs hold the promise of alfresco meals. At dusk lanterns light the scene, and the garden is the ideal place to be on a summer evening.

RIGHT It is easy to understand why Monet was so drawn to scenes like this – the floating flowers, the reflections and the wildlife all invite you to linger, observe or just relax.

healing plants, were places where they could contemplate their mortality as they cultivated cures to alleviate the suffering of the sick. At one end of the abbey building there was often a semi-circular garden called a paradise, which supplied flowers to decorate the altars and chapels.

Each contains elements that you may like to include in your own garden. The symbolically significant shapes and materials used in a Zen garden would be appropriate in a contemporary urban environment, the rills and reflecting pools of a Persian garden are ideal for a formal setting, while the healing herbs of a physic garden will fit in well to a country garden. In each case they will help set the mood and aid quiet thoughts.

Relaxation is less demanding – it can be found in a deckchair, on a hammock slung lying on the grass looking up at the sky or in the company of friends sitting around a table. Anywhere, in fact, you feel comfortable enough to forget your day-to-day worries and take a bit of time out.

With a little thought the same spot can be an aid to both contemplation and relaxation. Anyone who has walked around their own garden at dawn will know that the atmosphere is entirely different then to later in the day – so different that sometimes it is hard to believe that you are in the same garden. It becomes a place of mystery in the early half-light with creatures abroad that you will not see later. If you have never experienced this, it is worth making the effort – you will see the garden in a fresh light

ABOVE A length of wood tied to a rope and hung from a tree makes a simple swing – it invites both children and adults to stop and play.

OPPOSITE A Georgian-style metal bench is a good choice for a town garden. Surrounded by lavender, with a climbing rose on the wall behind and lime trees either side, this is a spot to bask in the sunshine or relax with a drink in the evening.

(literally) and have a sense of just how peaceful and mindful a place it can be.

In the same way that the garden looks different at different times of day, you can create areas which are used in a variety of ways throughout the day. A quiet moment of contemplation can be experienced standing next to a pond watching the reflections of the clouds pass across its surface, while later on it is the perfect spot in which to relax with a book. A summerhouse or pavilion at the end of the garden can be a foreign land for adventurous children, a relaxing place for a companionable tea party in the afternoon and an escape from the hurly-burly of family life in the evening. This type of building, whether it be summerhouse or shed, pavilion or temple, should be situated far enough away from the house to ensure that it fulfils its function as a refuge. Too close and you will be tempted back into domesticity, or it will become an annexe of the house with everyone congregating there just when you try to snatch a quiet moment.

In the centre of old Amsterdam, all the 17th-century houses that line the canals of the Grachtengordel have garden houses at the farthest point from the house. Some are

LEFT This charming summerhouse is a home from home with its pretty paintwork, mixture of furniture and potted plants on the windowsills. Its appearance belies its origins as a garden shed. A summerhouse should always be well removed from the house – a place to go to and get away from the rest of the family, to share a secret or to enjoy in solitude.

Try and find room for a swing. Remember when you were a child how you used to go and sit on the swing when you had something to think about? It works just as well when you are an adult.

grand stone affairs with intricate carvings and marble floors, others are built from wood with decorative fretwork embellishments, while elsewhere the tradition continues with modern buildings beyond the flower-filled gardens. The uses of the buildings are as varied as the styles of their architecture, but what they have in common is that they are removed from the influence of domestic life and as such can be used as places of refuge.

Treehouses have traditionally been children's territory, but increasingly adults are having them built for themselves. Very different from the dens fashioned from old planks and crates that I remember from my childhood, some are proper rooms perched in the boughs like the Swiss Family Robinson's treetop eyrie, with chairs and tables, beds and even electricity and running water in some instances. Others restrict themselves to being lofty

lookouts, but either way, they offer a perfect opportunity to relax and recapture the excitement of childhood adventures.

So, too, do swings and hammocks; after all relaxation is as much about fun as it is about rest, so even if children don't often use your garden, try and find room for a swing – not a modern, playground swing but something old-fashioned to hang from a tree. Visiting children will be delighted and it is guaranteed to be well used by adults, too. Remember when you were a child how you used to go and sit on the swing when you had something to think about? It works just as well when you are an adult. Hammocks are a source of entertainment as well as ultimate relaxation. The entertainment is to be had from watching others trying to get into the hammock without falling out; sitting up in a hammock is neither easy nor recommended. The relaxation comes when they succeed. Sling a hammock in a secluded corner of the garden where you will be left undisturbed.

OPPOSITE These days treehouses are as likely to be built for adults as for children. They offer a fresh perspective on the garden – or even life! Before you build, you should check with your neighbours if it overlooks their garden, and in some areas planning permission is required.

ABOVE Removable covers and synthetic fillings are best for outdoor cushions. If they are left out overnight they can be washed and dried without damage.

Finding peace and quiet when you live in the city is a far harder prospect than in the countryside, but even a small roof garden, balcony or terrace can lift you above the hustle and bustle and provide an outside space for those who spend most of their lives indoors. The ideal arrangement in this type of raised urban garden is a low screen of planting that gives shelter and privacy when you are sitting down but does not obscure the view. In the absence of rolling hills and fields, this sense of space is a valuable commodity and becomes a beautiful sight when everything is lit up at night.

An old-fashioned verandah or a terrace next to the house may provide the occasional quiet moment for contemplation early in the morning or in the evening, but its primary function is as an informal gathering place. It is usually positioned to make the best of the climate. Sheltered, sometimes shady and certainly convenient, it is where family and friends get together for alfresco meals, to exchange confidences or enjoy a siesta in a comfy chair. Pots of favourite plants often find a home here, and tending them, especially if they are sweetly scented, is a relaxing pastime for those who find it hard to sit down for long.

A garden that is used for contemplation and relaxation needs plenty of places to sit. These include solitary chairs in secluded corners where you can think deep thoughts, benches in sunny spots surrounded by scented plants where you can exchange confidences or sit in companionable silence, and folding chairs that can be easily moved to take advantage of a patch of sun or shade depending on the season. Seats carefully positioned around the garden will reveal the best views to visitors, or encourage them to pause alongside a pond or other garden feature that is worthy of closer examination.

OPPOSITE A desk with a perfect view – cool, uncluttered, conducive to thought, the scene provides restful relief from work but is not full of distraction. When working at home it is all too easy to be diverted from the task at hand.

ABOVE This London roof terrace uses a screen of elaeagnus for privacy and as a windbreak. This is not allowed to grow tall enough to hide the view, which has its own charm, especially at night when the buildings are illuminated.

RIGHT A quiet bench well away from the house is a refuge from interruptions and all the demands of life. It's a place to think, dream or read (although a cushion might be advisable).

BELOW A simple wooden bench tucked away in the corner of this building offers privacy, concealment or shelter from the rain.

OPPOSITE A rustic chair and table blend in perfectly in this woodland clearing. They are robust enough to be left out all year round, so they are always available for an impulse visit.

Comfortably cushioned chairs in a summerhouse might persuade you to take shelter there instead of retreating indoors during summer showers – there is something delightfully frivolous about sitting somewhere like this waiting for the rain to stop instead of rushing inside.

Eating outdoors is one of life's great pleasures, providing that it is a comfortable experience. Ideally the table and chairs should be close to the kitchen – that way it's easy to be spontaneous and decide on the spur of the moment to decamp outside. The idea of eating at the far end of the garden may appeal, but the reality is that someone has to carry everything there and back, a chore that is not always conducive to domestic harmony. Have an occasional picnic there instead and leave the table and chairs somewhere more convenient.

Because it needs to withstand the weather, most garden furniture is a compromise between comfort and durability, which means that a good supply of cushions is essential. Keep a large basket of them in the porch, summerhouse or shed so that they are easy to bring out and put away. Make sure they are washable, and if you live somewhere where the winters are cold or damp, bring the cushions indoors and store them in a warm place or they will become musty. Small details like these may seem rather trifling, but when they are a cause of irritation or argument they can interfere with the peaceful atmosphere of the garden.

Special places

Within every garden there are places that are invested with meaning, places where an object, a plant or a view has particular significance for the gardener. It can be a memento recalling love or loss, a work of art or a even a tree grown from a seed.

What makes a place special? It is your relationship with that place and how that connection was forged. Maybe it brought you comfort in adversity, calm when all around was in turmoil or joy in a troubled world. But it need not be the big experiences of life that make this link, sometimes it is the private pleasures: finding the first snowdrop in midwinter, watching a fledgling fly or picking and tasting the first peas you have ever grown – simple things that can tie you to a particular spot in the garden. When life gets complicated you can go to that special spot, or visit it in your imagination and feel comforted.

A special space can be something private and exclusive to you or a shared experience. When it is shared it can be a way of communicating to others how you feel about them or your garden, but be discriminating about who you choose to do this with or you may risk spoiling the place or the relationship.

It may be that your special space needs no embellishment, but sometimes it is nice to celebrate the relationship by adding your own decorative touches wto an otherwise low-key spot. 'Found' objects gathered from around the garden often work best; they have an

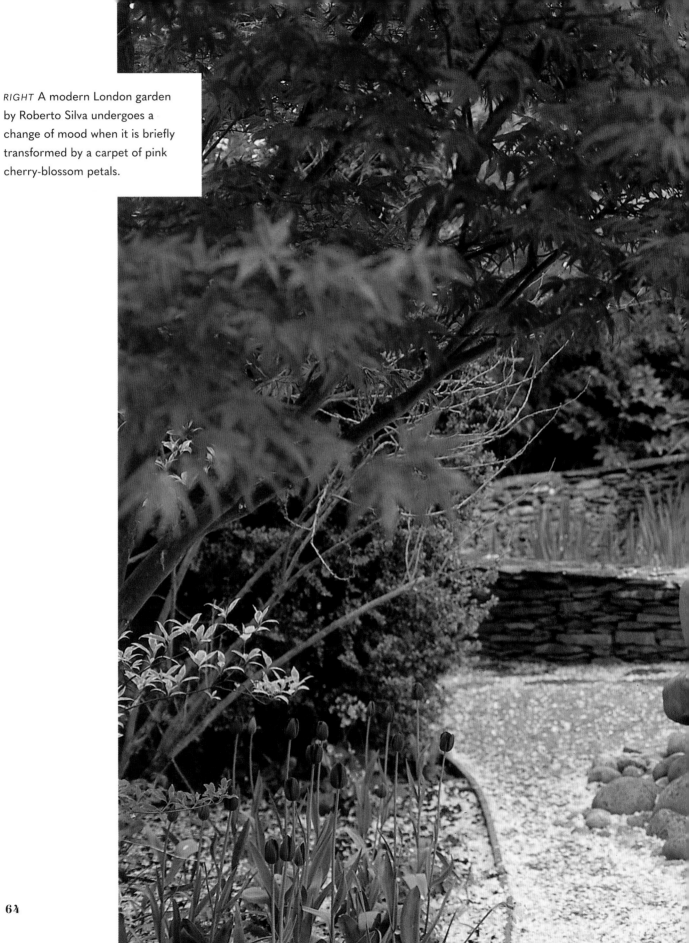

RIGHT A modern London garden
by Roberto Silva undergoes a
change of mood when it is briefly
transformed by a carpet of pink
cherry-blossom petals.

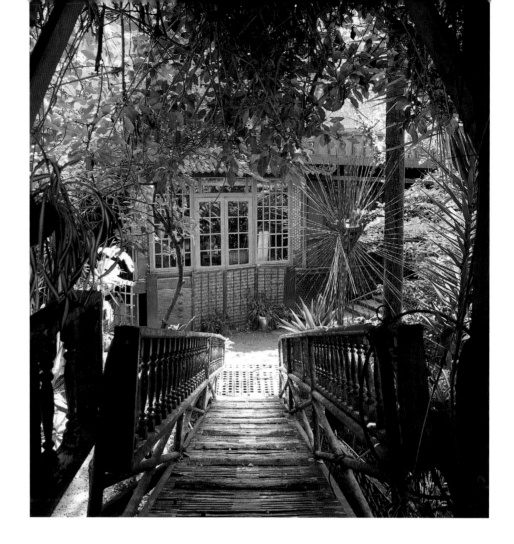

OPPOSITE In the garden of Mirabel Osler, a mirrored archway creates the illusion of another garden – the ultimate special space – visible but not attainable. By angling the mirror so that it is not approached straight on the illusion is sustained.

RIGHT In a Beverly Hills garden, weathered balustrading reclaimed from Rudolph Valentino's former home Falcon's Lair is used to great effect as the railings for an atmospheric walkway that leads to a summerhouse at the bottom of the garden.

Works of art give structure to a place and act as anchor points that focus the attention. Over time, their beauty changes and transforms as they become weathered and they settle into their surroundings.

integrity and a sense of rightness that can be missing from imported materials. This type of decoration is reminiscent of the cave paintings, dolmens and menhirs of our earliest ancestors.

On the other hand, a work of art by a favourite artist may find a perfect home in your special place. It can be fitting to mark an unexpected windfall or work well done with this type of memorial. Make sure whatever you add has some significance, or it will be little more than furniture – filling the space but adding nothing to its meaning. Works of art, when appropriate, give structure to a place

and act as anchor points that focus the attention. Over time, their beauty changes and transforms as they become weathered and settle into their surroundings.

If works of art are beyond your means or do not appeal, there are several less costly alternatives worth considering. Reclamation yards are filled with all manner of extraordinary items in all sorts of materials, from broken columns to old metalwork, which can add character and a sense of history to your garden. Sometimes a stroll around one of these will present you with the perfect object at a knock-down price.

ABOVE A treasured memento of travel to a faraway place, this fine sculpture is a true work of art. A piece of this quality needs to be carefully positioned.

ABOVE RIGHT Garden art does not need to be priceless. This wind chime was made by hanging flattened spoons and a bell from fishing line.

RIGHT A magnificent urn fashioned from slate by sculptor Joe Smith is an object of wonder and great beauty. It needs no embellishment, so the surrounding planting has been kept low.

OPPOSITE Designer Ivan Hicks created a woodland work of art by piling a cairn of stones on top of a reclaimed stone frame.

*A curving path that leads you on, a half-hidden wicket gate
in a hedge or a door left ajar in a wall all invite exploration.
A sense of mystery enlivens a garden and promises revelation.*

Mirrors can be used to create the illusion
of a larger space or another garden through an
arch or doorway, especially if the mirror is slightly
angled so that visitors do not see their reflections
as they approach it. Mirrors also bring light to
otherwise dark areas, similarly stained-glass panels
positioned so that the sun can shine through
the jewelled colours will transform a space into
something utterly magical.

One of the most seductive features a garden
can possess is a door in a wall. It harks back
to childhood and the world of the imagination
conjured up by books like *The Secret Garden*
by Frances Hodgson Burnett and the Narnia
stories by C. S. Lewis. Some years ago I had the
experience of being lost in the depths of the
Somerset countryside; arriving at the outskirts of
an unknown village I stopped next to a wall to get
my bearings. Looking up from my map I noticed
a door in the wall which bore the simple legend
'To the Garden'. Feeling like a character from
Alice's Adventures in Wonderland I felt compelled
to investigate, excited yet also a touch fearful of
what I might find beyond. I'm pleased to report
that I neither fell down a well nor encountered
the Red Queen. Instead I found myself in the
garden that had once belonged to the great
plantswoman, Margery Fish – a memorable visit
that has forged a special relationship between
me and that place.

Simple touches are often more effective than
grand decorative flourishes. When framing a view,
it is the view, not the frame, that should draw the

OPPOSITE A door left ajar is an invitation to explore further. There is always a sense of excitement and anticipation about what might lie beyond.

ABOVE An archway leads from the garden into the meadow, drawing you forward to discover the wild and sunlit landscape that lies beyond.

RIGHT After you pass through the archway, it is echoed by a curving pair of rustic poles that marks the beginning of a grassy path winding through the wildflower meadow. The makeshift arch perfectly frames the distant tree, which might otherwise go unremarked.

LEFT A grass pathway, its margins softened by plants, leads to a wooden doorway, tempting you to explore further. Even if the door does not conceal a hidden garden, by its very existence it makes the space seem bigger.

OPPOSITE At the end of this path a quirky, homemade fence and arch give the furthest part of the garden a sense of enclosure without totally concealing the space from the rest of the garden. A solid fence would make the garden feel smaller.

attention. The frame provides an appropriate setting, but if it is unnecessarily elaborate it will act as a distraction. Subtlety deepens the experience. A curving path that leads you on to a unseen destination, a half-hidden wicket gate in a hedge or a door left ajar in a wall all invite exploration, and the pleasure and surprise at the discovery of a wonderful view or a hidden garden is all the greater for the journey that has been taken. A sense of mystery enlivens a garden and promises revelation.

Plants, too, make a vital contribution to a special space. They can be used to enclose, conceal, frame or surround your chosen spot. Their colours, textures and fragrances help define and emphasize the mood. A shady garden can be enlivened by drifts of white flowers that bring light and contrast – a wooded glade becomes romantic when softly illuminated by pale foxgloves and martagon lilies. A sunny corner, where fragrant lavender and rosemary surround a stone seat and creeping thymes grow among the flagstones, will be filled with colour and a heady fragrance.

Climbing plants that are allowed to clothe a wall and curtain an archway offer both concealment and discovery. Sometimes a single plant is all you need, especially in

OPPOSITE An old stone column hints at the possibility of an earlier, more formal garden, lost long ago. The trimmed topiary counterpoints the air of abandon, showing that the effect is intentional.

BELOW LEFT A beautifully simple wooden bench carved with a couple's initials transforms this wooded glade into a trysting place.

a contemporary garden with a minimalist aesthetic – a rustling bamboo that moves gently in the wind, an architectural plant that throws dramatic shadows on a painted wall or a solitary tree to soften the stones that surround it. The right plant in the right place.

Sometimes it is the plants themselves that make the space special – it might be a rose grown from a cutting from your childhood garden, a souvenir of a lovely holiday or a tree raised from a seed by one of your children who has now grown up and left home. Plants like this are loaded with significance and create a living bond between you and your outdoor space.

My own garden is full of such plants and when I walk around it I find myself reliving my past experiences and thinking of friends and family. There is the olive tree I bought back from Tuscany as a sapling, now ten feet/three metres tall, and a blue perennial cornflower known by all the family as 'Mrs. Bottomley' in honour of the person who gave us the first small plant from her garden. Most significant of all for me is a perfect, richly scented pink rose, which was reputedly grown from a cutting taken from a rose that grew on the poet Omar Khayyam's grave. I planted it originally in the garden of the first home I lived in as an adult and when I moved it was potted up and brought with me. It then spent twenty years in that pot travelling from place to place, and it is only now that I have at last found my special space that I feel ready once more to plant it in my garden.

Tranquillity
FOR THE
SENSES

Detail is as important in the mindful garden as design and layout. Choosing the right colours and textures and observing the effect of light and shade help set the mood. Let your emotions be your guide – if a colour, a texture or a play of light calms and pleases you it will contribute to the overall effect of the garden.

RIGHT *Stipa tenuissima* is one of the most tactile grasses, with its soft green hairlike foliage tinged bronze at the tips. Its texture is reminiscent of doll's hair. The haze of grass contrasts nicely here with the knapweed.

Soothing colours

The mindful garden requires a subtle and restrained palette, where plants blend
in harmonious drifts. Cool, soft or pastel tones will complement the calm mood.

The gentle, soothing presence of green is at the core of the mindful garden. The myriad shades of the foliage form the backdrop and supplies the supporting cast for the flowers, their delicate beauty becoming all the more apparent when set in a sea of green. It is a constantly metamorphosing colour, from the fresh acid greens of spring through the dusky greens of summer to the transformations of autumn and the rich, glossy leaves of evergreens and glaucous hues of conifers in winter. In his poem 'The Garden', the poet Andrew Marvell (1621–1678) wrote of 'a green thought in a green shade'. Nearly four hundred years later we still feel the pull of that phrase, and like Marvell will often seek out a cool, bosky corner of the garden in which to think quiet thoughts.

In the peaceful flower garden too, green often predominates, while the other colours which feature are chosen to be complementary rather than contrasting. Whites, creams, pinks, blues and purples all blend together harmoniously, and soft yellows have their place as well, but contrasting colours such as oranges, bright reds and bright yellows should be avoided as they intensify the greens and make the effect less calming. A garden with little or no foliage, or one where foliage is secondary to the flowers, may have impact, but it is seldom peaceful in its mood. Think of the bulb fields of Holland where great

ABOVE FROM LEFT The pink blooms of this alpine clematis (*Clematis macropetala*) are an unusual sight in early spring. Less popular than its green cousin, purple basil has a rich, dark colouring that makes it worth growing. White agapanthus grows well in a container.

OPPOSITE At the foot of a hedge, the long grass is left untrimmed to allow the alliums and cow parsley to bloom around a flowering Judas tree (*Cercis siliquastrum*).

gashes of colour transect the landscape, or carpet bedding schemes with their hectic patterns – both attract attention, but neither soothes the eye.

If this all sounds rather too wishy-washy for your taste, don't despair. Although the palette may be restricted, the range of shades is not, and there is plenty of opportunity to use wonderfully rich colours. Combining deep shades of purple and pink with strong blues creates an intensely colourful tapestry, and softer plantings always look more interesting when some dark tones are included.

Weaving the plants among one another blends the colours like an Impressionist painter. This is most easily done by planting in irregular-shaped drifts that consist of uneven numbers of plants – three, five or seven for example. This effect can work well even in a formal garden. Box edging or other features provide the structure and definition for the soft planting within. Such planting, however, is not suited to a symmetrical arrangement and can easily look messy, especially if a plant or two fails and leaves the whole display looking somewhat gap-toothed.

Colour-themed gardens are popular and they can be very restful. The White Garden at Sissinghurst is a good example – with its white, silver and grey plants, it is a serene and inspiring place to sit. Even though the palette is restricted, there is an enormous variety of subtly different colours which blend together to create the overall picture. Remember that rigid adherence to your chosen colour theme creates blandness in the garden, and neurosis in the gardener!

PREVIOUS PAGE LEFT The intense purple of morning glory is one of the most appealing colours in the garden, and its transience adds to its beauty.

PREVIOUS PAGE RIGHT As flowers open their colours change; the cerise of this unfurling allium will soften.

BELOW The flowering habit of *Primula vialii* resembles that of a wild orchid with its succession of tiny flowers opening over many weeks. The rust-coloured cone at the top conceals the unopened buds.

Depending on the time of day, colours can look very different – blues and whites tend to look harsh or washed out at midday, yet at dawn and dusk they take on a luminous quality that is quite hypnotic in its effect. This type of transformation is at the heart of the mindful garden.

OPPOSITE The starburst flower heads of alliums last many weeks in the garden and the seedheads that follow are just as decorative.

ABOVE The canna lily is a tender plant, but nurture it for the striking colours of its architectural leaves and its bright flower spikes.

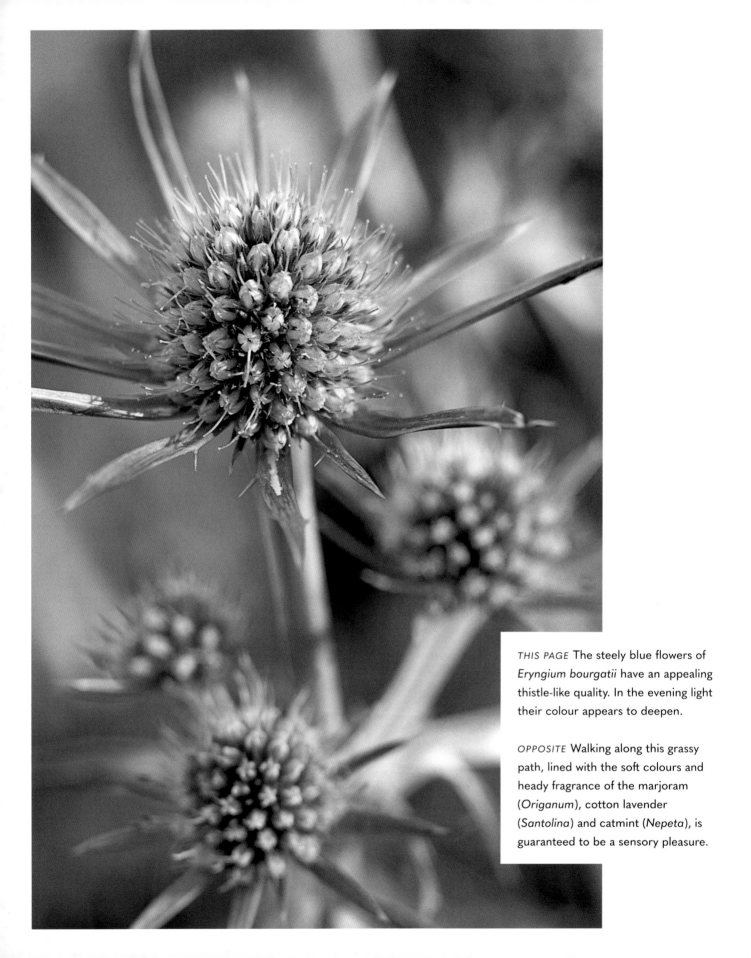

THIS PAGE The steely blue flowers of
Eryngium bourgatii have an appealing
thistle-like quality. In the evening light
their colour appears to deepen.

OPPOSITE Walking along this grassy
path, lined with the soft colours and
heady fragrance of the marjoram
(*Origanum*), cotton lavender
(*Santolina*) and catmint (*Nepeta*), is
guaranteed to be a sensory pleasure.

RIGHT Delicate *Ammi majus* resembles cow parsley and is usually grown as a hardy annual.

BELOW White flag irises flower briefly but gloriously.

BELOW RIGHT Flowering grasses such as *Eriophorum angustifolium* have a subtle beauty.

OPPOSITE The hues of *Astrantia major* range from white to pink and red. The paler colours show up well in light shade.

The gentle presence of green is at the core of the mindful garden. It is a constantly metamorphosing colour, from the fresh acid greens of spring to the the rich, glossy leaves of evergreens in winter.

PLANTS FOR SOOTHING COLOURS

Agapanthus

Allium

Ammi majus (bishop's flower)

Astrantia major (masterwort)

Cerinthe

Clematis macropetala (alpine clematis)

Digitalis purpurea f. albiflora (white foxglove)

Eryngium bourgatii (sea holly)

Helleborus orientalis (hellebore)

Hesperis matronalis (sweet rocket)

Hydrangea

Ipomoea (morning glory)

Iris

Lavandula (lavender)

Nepeta (catmint)

Nigella (love-in-a-mist)

Origanum (marjoram)

Papaver somniferum (opium poppy)

OPPOSITE LEFT The brilliant green of young *Matteuccia struthiopteris* fronds unfold in a display of natural beauty.

OPPOSITE RIGHT Ferns such as this *Dryopteris dilatata* are perfect plants for a shady woodland garden.

ABOVE A leafy path edged with hedges and overhung by trees draws you deeper and deeper into the garden.

LEFT A green-painted bench echoes the surrounding foliage and grass. This subtle hue is ideal for a peaceful garden.

Soothing textures

Every plant and every surface within the garden has a texture and a relationship with its surroundings. Soothing textures are more about that relationship than the feel of a leaf or the finish of a stone.

An easy way to understand the relationship between different textures is to look at a Zen garden. Its timeless and peaceful beauty is an enduring legacy of the Buddhist monks who created it. By creating symbolic gardens that represented the pathway to enlightenment, the monks were able to explain the principles of Zen to their followers.

Each rock, tree or shrub is placed with infinite care and has special meaning. A rock placed horizontally can represent the sky, vertically the earth, or depending on shape or position, it may be an island or even an animal. A clipped shrub symbolizes billowing clouds and the use and form of small pebbles, gravel and sand help create an atmosphere conducive to meditation.

Each element is pared-down, simple and refined. Change is not necessary. There is nothing superfluous or frivolous, no giving way to the temptation to include a favourite flower or put a seat in a sunny corner. In the Zen garden everything has added meaning and looking at it can be a profound experience.

This doesn't mean that every mindful garden should follow the Zen model, but it can help you to reach an understanding of how to combine elements successfully

ABOVE FROM LEFT There is a pleasing contrast as a wooden deck gives way to concrete stepping stones and rounded pebbles. Sometimes all you need to highlight texture is a variation in size. The linear design of the etched glass window and plain panelled walls is emphasized by decking.

OPPOSITE Like fragments of paving from an ancient ruin, these stones have more presence than conventional slabs.

RIGHT Very much an outdoor room, this garden has been furnished and decorated with contrasting textures – a carpet of gravel, differing surfaces on the painted walls, concrete sofas with matting cushions and a bamboo table. The tree in the corner is the only living thing in this garden.

when you mix planting and hard landscaping. Once more this is an aspect of garden design that needs to involve your emotional response. If the juxtaposition of two different textures feels right then it usually is; if, on the other hand, you feel uncomfortable, then it may be a sign that you need to try some other solutions.

The obvious way to check how you react to textures is to touch them. Hold a smooth stone in your hand and notice how you turn it round and round, pick up a handful of gravel and pour it from one hand to the other, run some sand through your fingers – these are tactile experiences and will help you understand how you relate to the materials. Not all responses are positive; some people hate sand (it reminds them of gritty sandwiches on the beach), while others dislike gravel surfaces because they love to walk barefoot in the garden. By exploring your responses to the different textures before you embark on your garden, you can create an environment tailored to your own preferences.

But the mindful garden does not consist solely of rounded stones and velvety leaves. It is the relationship of one thing with another that is important, and here a contrast often works better than textures or shapes that are too similar. Think of a border where all the plants have similar leaves, or a garden where every surface is the same – the effect is more likely to be boring than soothing.

There are words which describe texture or shape that have the power to soothe – words like round, curved, smooth, undulating. They can be used as guides to some of the textures to include in your garden, especially the surfaces – paving, steps, walls and water features. The materials that

are used for these elements in the garden are most successful when they are sympathetic
to their surroundings. Polished concrete, slate and metal are perfectly at home in an urban
setting, while rustic timber, weathered brick and stone blend seamlessly into a country garden.
This sensitivity to the surroundings is part of what makes a garden peaceful – jarring notes
should be avoided. Imagine a country garden where a blue glass mulch has been spread
on a border, or a city garden where a cottage garden arch, complete with roses, is placed
in minimalist surroundings. Eccentric maybe, but definitely not soothing.

The materials traditionally used for building in your area can also be used as a guide. If the
houses are built of granite, a garden that features sandstone will look out of place – think of
the two materials alongside one another and it will give you an idea of whether your choice is
appropriate. In this instance, slate looks much better with granite than sandstone. When the
material is right, its texture becomes less significant. And once the hard landscaping has been
resolved, it becomes much easier to choose suitable plants.

There are as many plant textures as there are plants; the differences, sometimes obvious,
sometimes subtle, are as important as the variation of colour within a garden. Read through a
list of plant descriptions and texture is a key element, whether soft and hairy, plump and fleshy,

OPPOSITE LEFT On this low-maintenance urban terrace, textures dominate and plants take a back seat. Irregular-shaped blocks of York stone are bedded in smooth pebbles. The concrete border has a sunken recess for a barbecue/grill or fire.

OPPOSITE RIGHT There is a monumental feeling to this stone wall with its rough-hewn surfaces, but the area does not feel closed in; intersected by the pillars of stone, the wall becomes far more significant. The simple grass carpet seems entirely appropriate; any plants would detract from its power.

BELOW Bluestone and pink bricks compose this small, square terrace, which leads to a gravelled area.

RIGHT The curled tips of hosta leaves push through pebbles and stones. At present the hard landscaping is more evident than the plant, but once the leaves are open they will dominate.

PLANTS FOR SOOTHING TEXTURES

Artemisia 'Powis Castle' – ferny foliage

Ballota pseudodictamnus – woolly foliage

Bamboos – ferny foliage

Eryngium alpinum – tickly/prickly, ferny leaves

Eschscholzia (California poppy) – silky petals and ferny foliage and flowers

Ferns – curling fronds

Foeniculum vulgare (fennel) – ferny foliage

Hosta – bold, ribbed leaves

Papaver somniferum (opium poppy) – silky flowers and ferny foliage

Pelargonium tomentosum – hairy, ferny foliage

Romneya coulteri – papery flowers and ferny foliage

Salix caprea (pussy willow) – velvety catkins and bold foliage

Salvia officinalis (sage) – bold, rough leaves

Sedum – bold, fleshy leaves

Stachys lanata – bold, woolly leaves

Stipa tenuifolia – hairy

Thalictrum – ferny foliage

Verbascum olympicum – bold, woolly leaves and flower spikes

LEFT An informal path has steps made from salvaged railway sleepers/railroad ties. Plants grow and self-seed happily in the gravel.

OPPOSITE This is a garden full of contrasting textures. A decking boardwalk leads across a dry garden of bold, linear plants such as palms, grasses and phormiums. However, behind this carefully set scene a conventional garden intrudes rather uncomfortably.

deeply ridged, prickly, fuzzy or thorny. You will respond to the texture as much as you do to the other details.

When walking around the garden, notice how often your hand reaches out to touch a flower, stroke a leaf or feel the smoothness of bark. Your brain may not always register what you are doing, but in the same way that stroking a pet induces calm, this tactile tour of the garden is a soothing experience. In most gardens the plant textures are incidental, but when you are making a mindful garden you can consciously select your favourite surfaces, barks or patinas. They will sustain the garden long after flowers have faded. In the same way that the blending of colours creates patterns in the garden, so the combining and blending of textures gives rhythm and variation to the planting.

Viewed from a distance, texture is about shape and outline – after all touch cannot be experienced from afar. But interesting outlines and contrasting shapes will draw you closer until you are near enough for a truly tactile experience. This is where texture becomes really significant. Surfaces – of leaves, stems, bark, fruit and even flowers – gain their character as much from their texture as their colour, and in gardens where colour is restricted, texture is essential to avert monotony. Describe a leaf as puckered, ribbed, rough, smooth, shiny, matte, prickly, thorny or furry and you quickly realize how very different they are one from another, not just in appearance but in the effect that they have on the general

THIS PAGE Different hard
landscaping materials make an
interesting pattern on this garden
floor. In the foreground the linear
planks, set in stones, draw you
further into the garden, where
the curving setts lead you to either
side of the central area laid with
simple paving slabs.

FAR LEFT This wall, made from Welsh slate using drystone walling techniques, is both beautiful and practical. It snakes its way through the garden dividing different areas, its rough texture a contrast to its shape.

LEFT The smooth finish of the timber deck contrasts with the rough slate and mixed stones, which are carpeted with blossom.

BELOW This patterned path in a herb garden has a wonderful patina of age. Natural materials such as stone, brick and tile become more subtle as the years pass.

view. Shiny surfaces advance, appearing closer than they actually are, while matte finishes have the opposite effect and tend to recede.

There are three basic shapes of foliage in the garden – bold, linear and ferny. Bold encompasses the big leaves like *Fatsia*, *Gunnera*, *Rheum* and Hosta; these sorts of leaves are popular in tropical or architectural planting schemes. Linear includes sword-like foliage and many of the grasses, while ferny covers the softer shapes including, of course, ferns. By combining these shapes in your planting you create instant interest. If you still find it difficult to grasp the impact that texture has on planting, try taking black-and-white photographs of your garden. By removing the distraction of colour, texture comes to the fore. If the pictures all look rather monotonous, this is an indication that you need to introduce more contrasting textural effects.

Bold foliage plants bring substance to the garden, but scale and proportion also need to be considered. Including the grandest of these plants in a small garden can leave room for little else – fine if it is a simple, minimalist garden, but very limiting if it is not. Also bear in mind that some plants, such as *Gunnera*, die right down in winter, leaving very little evidence of their otherwise impressive presence. On a smaller scale, hostas provide some of the best bold foliage in the garden. Their large ridged, pleated or puckered leaves have a wonderful textural quality and the colour variations add further interest. They too have their limitations – they are a favourite food of slugs and snails, and their beautiful leaves can be reduced to lace where these pests are a problem. In such cases hostas are best grown in pots protected by copper tape or another deterrent.

Although not all linear plants are grasses they make up by far the largest group of plants, encompassing everything grassy from giant bamboos to the prettily compact *Festuca glauca*. Grass, in all its shapes and

forms, provides many of the most soothing textures in the garden. And not just the ornamental varieties either – think of your lawn and the pleasure to be gained from walking on it barefoot, or lying on your back looking up at the sky. Both are highly evocative experiences, often sending you back to your childhood and more carefree times. If you haven't done either in a long time, you are missing out on two of the simplest and purest pleasures to be found in the garden.

In recent years ornamental grasses have become increasingly popular with gardeners as informal planting has taken over from the ordered borders of the past. The relaxed, fluid effect of grasses is perfectly at home

OPPOSITE LEFT The cat's-tongue roughness
of sage leaves does not appeal to everyone.

OPPOSITE RIGHT AND THIS PAGE Succulents
beg to be touched. From the smallest to
the largest, their fleshy leaves are
irresistibly tactile. They store moisture
in their foliage, so will grow happily in arid
conditions such as the tops of gateposts,
or in shallow containers on tabletops. With
their modest demands they could easily be
overlooked, but close study reveals fantastic
variations in colour and texture.

in contemporary gardens, whether they are in an urban or rural setting. The fact that they are very easy to grow, undemanding and look wonderful throughout the year has also helped their popularity. Even in the dead of winter the dry stems and seedheads have a presence in the garden, especially when they are rimed with frost. They are important for wildlife, too – beneficial insects hibernate among the dry foliage and birds find valuable food in the seedheads. Leaving the grasses untrimmed fits in well with their correct care. They should be cut back, thinned or divided in spring rather than in the autumn. This will prevent them rotting, usually caused by water getting into the crown.

The third basic shape – ferny – naturally includes many ferns. Some ferns will grow happily in dry shade or other difficult situations and their delicate fronds contrast softly with the other, more architectural shapes. In sunny, open positions other plants with fern-like foliage are more appropriate – *Thalictrum, Artemisia, Eschscholzia,* and *Senecio cineraria* are just a few examples.

ABOVE LEFT The bronzy-red leaves and delicate purple flower heads of *Panicum virgatum* 'Shenandoah' make it a particularly appealing switch grass.

ABOVE RIGHT Stipa gigantea is the stateliest of grasses. It sends up a fountain of tall flowering stalks that turn golden bronze during summer.

OPPOSITE Briza maxima is commonly known as quaking grass, a perfect name for this delicate annual with ever-moving pendent seedheads. Their appearance invites you to run your fingers through them.

Hostas provide some of the best bold foliage in the garden. Their large ridged, pleated or puckered leaves have a wonderful textural quality and the colour variations add further interest.

It is useful to have lists of plants that fit into the different categories when you are planning your garden. One of the best ways to compile such a list is to visit a good garden centre and make a note of anything that appeals to you under the three headings bold, linear and ferny. Not only will this broaden your plant knowledge, but you will also have a clearer understanding of the different shapes, which are just as relevant whether you are looking at a tiny alpine or a sixteen-foot/five-metre bamboo.

As you make your choices, other categories and sub-categories will also become evident, and this is where texture really comes into play. Woolly-leaved plants like *Stachys lanata*, also known as lamb's or rabbit's ears, are irresistible – stroking their leaves is reminiscent of the feel of a favourite stuffed toy from childhood – while the tall mullein, *Verbascum olympicum*, has huge, bold, woolly leaves and flower spikes that bear golden flowers. While you are making your list, notice the plants that you touch and be sure to make a note of them too. Roses may be prickly, but their flower petals feel like silk. Sedums are usually bought for their bright autumn flowers and their ability to attract butterflies, but their cool, fleshy leaves are good to touch. Fennel is thought of as a culinary herb, but its ferny foliage looks wonderful in the flowerbed too, and brushing against it is pleasantly tickly. The textures in a mindful garden are as much about the tactile experience as they are about their appearance.

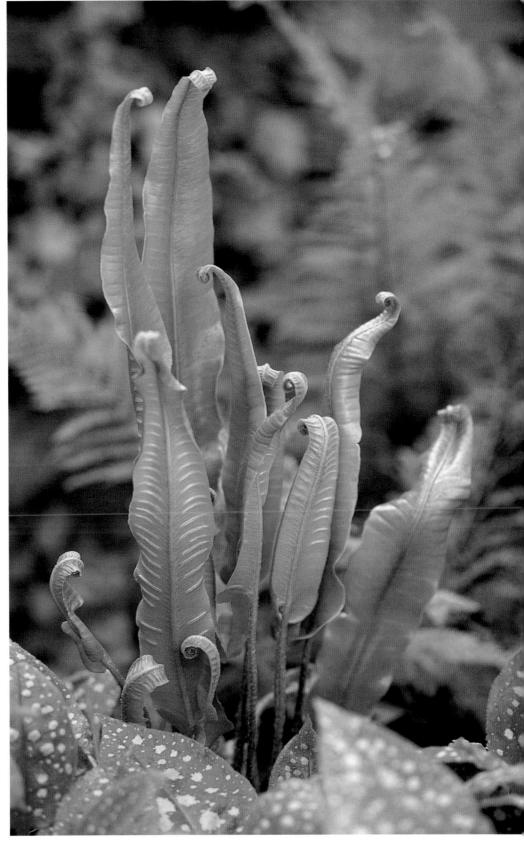

ABOVE Before young hosta leaves have opened fully, the contrasting colour and texture of their undersides is attractively revealed. Noticing these gradual transformations is one of the pleasures of the mindful garden.

LEFT Droplets of water hang on the ferny foliage of a fennel plant. Touching the plant when it is wet is a very different experience compared to when it is dry.

RIGHT The delicate unfurling leaves of the aptly named hart's-tongue fern (*Asplenium scolopendrium*) do not have the usual ferny foliage of the genus. Their shiny, leathery leaves have a strong linear quality.

Light and shade

The interplay of light and shade brings life to the garden and influences its mood. Light
changes constantly during the day, sometimes subtly and sometimes dramatically. Without
this variation the garden would be a less intriguing place and much of its magic would be lost.

Our eyes continually adjust to light, which means that
we are not always aware of how altered a view or even a
solitary flower can look in differing light conditions. In the
mindful garden it is helpful to observe these changes; it
is a pleasant activity and the understanding you gain may
lead you to make alterations or improvements. Watch
how light filters through plants onto the ground below,
creating shadow patterns; lie on your back under a tree
and see how sunlight illuminates the leaves; or sit next to
a pond and notice the play of light on water. If you have
never consciously noticed these things before it will be

a revelation. Use a camera as an impartial observer –
photographs taken of the same scene throughout the
day will reveal just how much light affects the results.

As the sun moves across the garden the quality of
light undergoes many transformations. At dawn the light
is soft and diffuse, starting quite cold and grey and
warming as the sun rises. This is the favourite time of day
for professional garden photographers – plants are fresh
and often dew-laden and there are no strong contrasts
or shadows. By noon, with the sun at its highest point,
the garden is full of light and shade. In direct light only

strongly coloured plants can stand the competition; others tend to look bleached or dulled. Shady areas lack definition, and here it is the pale colours that stand out from the crowd. With the approach of evening, shadows lengthen and the light softens once more, bathing the garden in a golden glow before fading to darkness.

The time of year and weather conditions also affect the quality of light. Even on a cloudy day there are variations – with thick cloud cover, the garden appears flat and one-dimensional, but as the cloud thins, shafts of light or dappling bring it back to life. In hot weather or where pollution is a problem the light is often hazy, while in sunny winter weather or after rain it can be crystal clear.

We cannot control the seasons or the weather, but light and shade can make a positive contribution to the garden. In the same way that lighting varies in a room – bright light for general use and soft light for intimate corners – arranging your garden so that it makes the best possible use of any light will make it a more welcoming place. A shady garden is more inviting when pools of dappled light illuminate its furthest reaches – they draw you towards them and give added depth. In the absence of direct light, a similar effect can be achieved with variegated foliage or white flowers. Conversely, sunny gardens need areas of shade for definition.

Light and shade are not only about how the garden looks, they are also about how it feels – in other words

Arranging your garden so that it makes the best possible use of any light will make it a more welcoming place.

OPPOSITE By twining pin-prick lights through a dark-leaved violet the colouring and droplets of moisture are brought into focus.

ABOVE Attractive glass lanterns are suspended at different levels from the branch of a tree, softly illuminating their surroundings. In the absence of specially designed glass lanterns, jam jars containing candles or night lights can be hung from wires for a similar effect.

RIGHT Torches are a wonderful way to light a garden on a special occasion. Pushed in among plants they can mark a path or simply act as decorations. Don't place them too close to path edges where clothing might catch light.

ABOVE Light filtering through a corkscrew willow creates a delicate tracery pattern on the water in a shallow galvanized trough. The stones highlight a subtle composition that might otherwise go unnoticed.

OPPOSITE The stone table on this terrace provides a cool, shady place to eat outdoor meals during the day. When evening comes the lanterns hanging above the table are lit to make the perfect spot to enjoy an alfresco dinner.

warmth and coolness. In a predominantly shady garden it is nice to have a patch of sun to bask in, and in a sunny garden the shade of a tree is a welcome retreat from soaring summer temperatures. These days most of us are more careful about exposure to the direct sun, especially around noon, but it is always pleasant to have somewhere to sit that catches the early morning or evening sun, even if it isn't close to the house. A distant bench positioned to catch the last rays of the setting sun will lure you outside to enjoy the peace and quiet of the garden. What better way to switch off after a hard day's work?

When buying a new home it is always worth asking the vendors where the sun rises and sets. Better still, try and visit the property at different times of day so that you can observe the light for yourself. When I bought my house,

FAR LEFT The play of light on the water of this natural stone swimming pool is far more enticing than it would be on a more conventional tiled pool. Areas of sun and shade around the pool provide relaxing spots for both sun-worshippers and shade-lovers alike.

LEFT A rustic lantern provides subtle lighting for a romantic outdoor dinner.

it wasn't until I moved in that I realized that, because it is situated on the wooded western slope of a valley, it loses the sun quite early in the evening. This means that it is wonderfully sheltered from the prevailing winds, but I do miss being able to wander round the garden in the warm evening sunshine.

The night-time garden is a place of darkness and mystery, so maybe it isn't surprising that many people are reluctant to venture out into their gardens after dark, even though they are so familiar during the day. Unfortunately the only artificial lighting that exists in most gardens is for security purposes, and it is about as flattering to its surroundings as the lighting in multi-storey car parks. Although installing well-designed garden lighting is quite an expensive process, its transforming effect is worth every penny. It can make an ordinary garden look quite magical, with washes and pools of light making the familiar seem quite new, and will greatly

A distant bench positioned to catch the last rays of the setting sun will lure you outside to enjoy the peace and quiet of the garden. What better way to switch off after a hard day's work?

extend the time you spend outdoors. Expert advice is to be recommended as this is a specialist subject. Solar lighting that needs no wiring is a sustainable option that is becoming more common, but in general the lamps give off less light than conventional alternatives. As the technology and the design improve, renewable power sources may open up many new possibilities for garden lighting.

On a much more modest scale, lanterns, candles, torches and fairy lights can be used to light alfresco meals or give the garden atmosphere on special occasions. Fairy lights can be twined through plants, around pergolas and up plant supports if there is an outdoor power source, but make sure you use lights that are safe outside. Floating candles transform a pond, and a candlelit table on the terrace is the perfect setting for a romantic meal. Chinese paper lanterns, hung from trees and illuminated by night lights, are both exotic and practical.

RIGHT **Perfectly positioned to catch the setting sun, this summerhouse is the ideal place to retreat to at the end of the day to enjoy a spell of peace and quiet.**

Lanterns, candles, torches and fairy lights can be used to light alfresco meals or give the garden atmosphere on special occasions.

OPPOSITE In this Los Angeles garden, fairy lights strung through the climbing plants on the pergola echo the city lights that twinkle far below. Crystal decorations have been hung from the pergola to catch the light. Comfortable chairs complete this inviting sitting area, a perfect spot for outdoor entertaining.

ABOVE A tiny courtyard comes to life at night when lit by night lights in Moroccan tea glasses, lanterns and a copper bowl.

RIGHT These glass candle holders are pretty and practical – the candles are safely contained and protected from draughts. The reflection of the flames creates changing patterns on the glass.

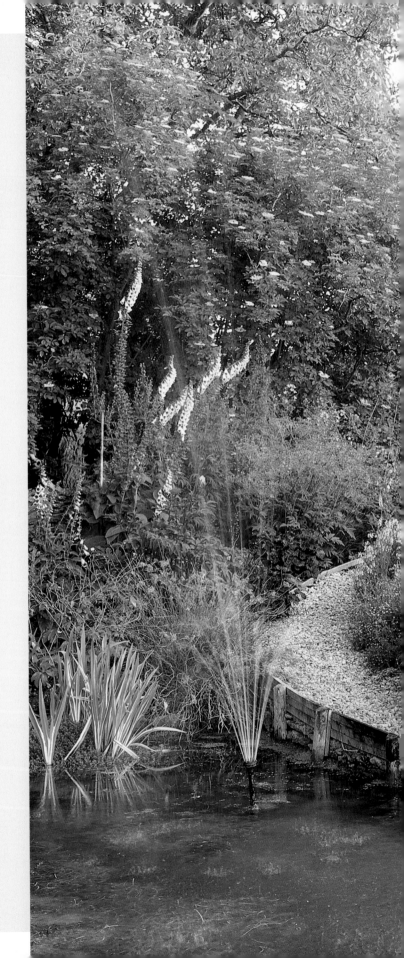

Scent AND
SOUND

Close your eyes in a mindful garden and its magic continues as your other senses are soothed and fine-tuned. The scent of perfumed flowers and aromatic herbs hangs in the air, and free of visual distraction, will envelop you. As you breathe in the fragrance you will become more aware of the soothing sounds around you – splashing water, rustling foliage or birdsong.

RIGHT The seat built into the bank next to this pond is an invitation to sit down and enjoy the view. The fountain could be improved – oddly positioned and standing proud of the water, it detracts from rather than adds to the scene. There are better ways to produce the sound of splashing water.

Fragrant plants

In our relationship with plants, fragrance is frequently as significant as appearance. There are plants of modest appearance that we grow purely for their scent – plants like mignonette, *Reseda odorata*, and night-scented stocks, *Matthiola bicornis* – while there are others that disappoint if they fail to smell as we expect. Roses or sweet peas with no scent are diminished by their lack of fragrance.

Our love affair with scented flowers has a long history. The Egyptians grew the sacred lotus for its voluptuous and narcotic scent. The Romans were so enamoured of the rose that they filled fountains with its petals, and the Persians invented the process of distillation to extract the essential oil from roses. During the Middle Ages in Europe, scented flowers were given as love tokens and some also had religious significance. The lily in particular was a symbol of fertility and purity and for centuries any painting of the Annunciation would include a lily held by the Madonna or an angel.

Our sense of smell works differently from the other senses because the olfactory nerves head straight for the emotions. Scent and memory are inextricably entangled, and a familiar fragrance will always recall past events. If you first smelled lavender in your grandmother's garden on a sunny day during a happy childhood holiday then lavender will recreate that feeling of happiness, while a heart broken under a honeysuckle will always associate its sweet fragrance with sadness.

RIGHT A cottage garden overflowing with flowers would be greatly diminished without fragrance. As beautiful as the roses are to look at, it isn't until we bury our noses in the blooms that we really respond to their beauty – even with our eyes closed.

PLANTS WITH FRAGRANT FLOWERS

WINTER *Hamamelis* (witch hazel)

Sarcococca humilis

Viburnum x bodnantense 'Dawn'

SPRING *Convallaria majalis* (lily of the valley)

Daphne odora 'Aureomarginata'

Mahonia aquifolium (Oregon grape)

SUMMER *Hesperis matronalis* (sweet rocket)

Jasmine, common or star

Lathyrus odoratus (sweet pea)

Lavandula (lavender)

Lilium candidum (Madonna lily)

Lonicera (honeysuckle)

Matthiola bicornis (night-scented stock)

Paeonia lactiflora (peony)

Philadelphus coronarius (mock orange)

Phlox paniculata (border phlox)

Reseda odorata (mignonette)

Rosa gallica var. *officinalis* and others

LEFT In a wildflower meadow a beautiful white rose scrambles through a neighbouring tree – evidence of a long-abandoned garden.

Before planting a scented garden it is interesting to check your own responses to the plants you have in mind. Scent is so subjective that other people's recommendations are not always appropriate.

The volatile oils that give flowers their fragrance are at their most concentrated in the plant early in the day. This is why roses that are gathered for perfumes are harvested at dawn. As the sun warms the flowers the oils evaporate and the fragrance is diffused into the surrounding air. When you walk through a sunny garden enjoying its sweet scents you are literally breathing in perfumed air.

Garden scents change with the seasons. Even in midwinter fragrant plants perfume the air. Witch hazel will stop you in your tracks, as will the scent of winter-flowering *Viburnum* and *Sarcococca*. Plant them close to a well-used path or terrace, unless you are in the habit of wandering round the garden in midwinter. In early spring the Oregon grape *Mahonia* and *Daphne odora* 'Aureomarginata' are deliciously scented, while lily of the valley is best picked and brought indoors to appreciate its lovely perfume. There are of course plenty of scented bulbs too – daffodils, jonquils, narcissus, hyacinths, and there are even tulips that have a sweet freesia scent, 'Ballerina' being one of the finest.

Once the summer arrives there are so many fragrances to choose from – the bubble-gum scent of the mock orange, the citrus scent of peony flowers, the musky fragrance of border phlox. As at the perfume counter of a department store you can take your pick of everything from the subtle to the overpowering.

Scented flowers are best appreciated in a sunny, sheltered garden – the sun concentrates the oils and shelter ensures that the scent hangs in the air rather than being blown away by the wind. The effect can be accentuated further by growing plants over bowers, arbours, arches and pergolas – all of which will trap the scent within them. A mixture of roses, honeysuckle, and jasmines – both *Jasminum officinale*, common jasmine, and the star jasmine, *Trachelospermum jasminoides*, will

ABOVE The pink and white blooms of this old-fashioned sweet pea are quite small but intensely fragrant. Fortunately many of the larger-flowered modern sweet peas are now having fragrance bred back into them, but it is always worth adding a few old varieties as well. To appreciate the scent of sweet peas you really need to grow them yourself – once picked the fragrance fades.

OPPOSITE Not all roses have a fine scent. The 'Peace' rose may have a perfect, delicate beauty, but sadly its fragrance does not match its looks.

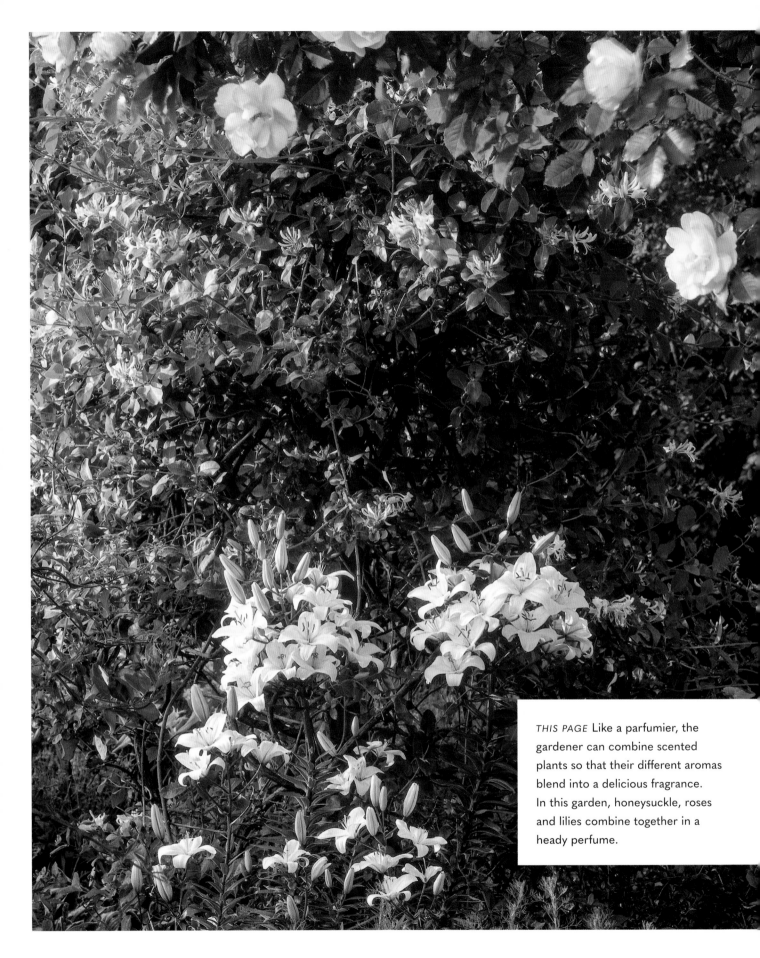

THIS PAGE Like a parfumier, the gardener can combine scented plants so that their different aromas blend into a delicious fragrance. In this garden, honeysuckle, roses and lilies combine together in a heady perfume.

Scented flowers are best appreciated in a sunny, sheltered garden - the sun concentrates the oils and shelter ensures that the scent hangs in the air rather than being blown away by the wind. Grow plants over bowers, arbours, arches and pergolas to trap the scent.

BELOW The flower of the French lavender *Lavandula stoechas* is very different in appearance to common lavender, but has a similar fragrance. 'Helmsdale' is a new cultivar with a striking dark burgundy flower.

provide long-lasting fragrance. Although their season is quite short, scented wisterias have a dramatic beauty, especially when the blooms hang down within a pergola. On a pathway fringed with fragrant plants, allow them to fall across its margins so that you brush against them and release their fragrance.

Of all scented flowers, roses are probably the most universally popular, but there is an enormous variability in their scent as well as their other qualities. The four roses considered best for the making of rose oil, and therefore the most fragrant, are 'Belle de Crécy', 'Louise Odier', 'Madame Isaac Pereire' and 'Roseraie de l'Haÿ', but it is worth remembering that these old varieties are not always repeat flowering and they can have rather untidy habits. Many modern roses are now bred to have the virtues of good scent, good growth habit and disease resistance.

Lavender is the quintessential cottage garden flower, but it needs the right conditions to grow well. It is a Mediterranean plant, so give it the full sun and good drainage it loves and it will thrive. It isn't the cold that kills lavender during the winter – it's the combination of cold and wet that is lethal. 'Hidcote' is the most popular variety – its deep colour and compact habit make it ideal for lining paths and growing in containers.

OPPOSITE A rose-covered arch and a lavender-lined pathway lead to a rustic bench – the perfect place to sit and drink in the scents that surround you.

RIGHT A grass path leads down the centre of a fragrant lavender walk. To keep it looking this good it is essential to trim the lavender as soon as the flowers start to fade – otherwise gaps will open up in the bushes and they will start to look leggy. Lavender is relatively short-lived, so it is a good idea to take cuttings from the second year onwards. You can never have too many lavender plants.

Herbs

Herbs are perfect companions in the peaceful garden. Their reassuring presence and aromatic qualities hark back to times when we had a much more direct connection with the plants we grew – they were our food and our medicine. For many of us herbs are now the only useful plants that we still cultivate and use as an everyday ingredient.

We respond very positively to the word 'herb', as indeed we do to many of the properties of the herbs themselves – for centuries they have been used to heal, soothe, cleanse and calm, as well as being essential and much-loved flavourings in our food. Our relationship with them is often reflected in their folk names – names like bee balm (*Melissa officinalis*), knitbone (*Symphytum officinale*), eyebright (*Euphrasia officinalis*), and feverfew (*Chrysanthemum parthenium*).

Although the modern herb garden is harvested mainly for culinary herbs or sometimes for ingredients used in the making of pot pourri and lavender bags, many of us also grow other herbs, a conscious or unconscious tribute to their historical importance as folk medicines. Herbs remain more than pleasantly fragrant plants that decorate our

gardens and enliven our foods. This does not mean though that they are all equally benign, and anyone cultivating herbs beyond the most well-known varieties should be familiar with their properties before doing anything other than admiring how they grow in the garden.

ABOVE FROM LEFT Although it is a nice idea to put a chair in the middle of a carpet of herbs, do it with caution – bees love these herbs as much as we do, so you risk being stung. Sage, so named for its reputation as a herb for improving memory, is now being used in the treatment of Alzheimer's disease. Rosemary tumbles over terracotta pots, conjuring up the colours and scent of Tuscany.

OPPOSITE Prostrate thymes and other low-growing herbs are perfect for the spaces between paving or on a terrace.

Enjoy herbs' aromatic qualities in the garden. Plant thyme and rosemary in between paving slabs and you will release their fragrance as you walk along the path.

LEFT A simple plank bench is a perfect excuse to linger among the herbs. The fragrance is always at its most intense after noon, when the volatile oils have evaporated from the herbs into the surrounding air.

ABOVE The distinctive flavour of caraway seeds is one of those tastes that you either love or hate. For some it evokes nostalgic memories of grandma's cakes.

If you are planning to lay out a herb plot in your mindful garden, it is important that you take into account the conditions which the different herbs require to grow well. The Mediterranean herbs – which include sage, rosemary, thyme, oregano and marjoram – need really good drainage and a hot sunny position. Think of their natural habitat – the arid, stony coastlines and hills of France, Italy and Greece – and you will realize that a deeply cultivated soil is far too rich a diet for them. They also hate to have their roots sitting in water, so lots of added grit is essential in all but the stoniest soils. However,

there are other herbs which welcome a moist soil and a degree of shade. Mint, parsley and lemon balm will all do better in fertile soil in a lightly shaded position. Mint and lemon balm need to be contained in some way or they will rapidly overwhelm their less rampant neighbours. Traditionally they were planted in buckets with a hole in the base. A modern equivalent is to cut the bottom out of a large pliable plastic pot, sink it in the ground with just the rim showing above soil level, and plant into this. Mint and lemon balm spread via runners along the top of the soil, so this method will keep them contained.

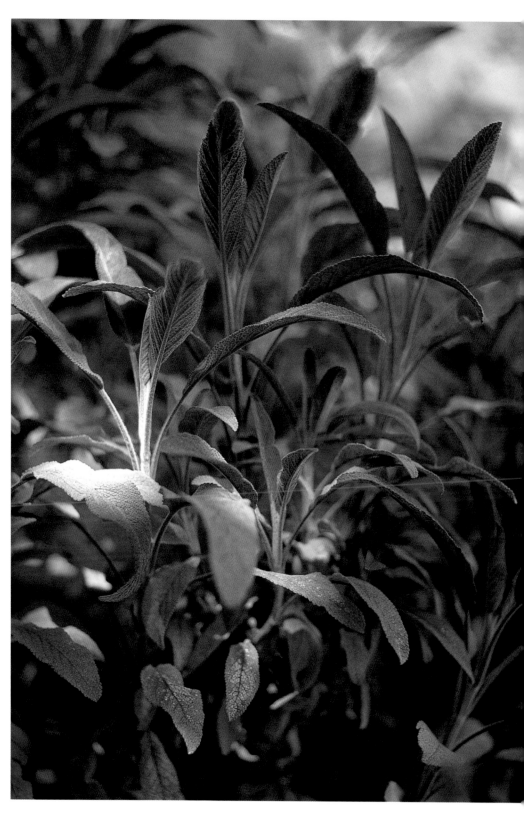

OPPOSITE Culinary thyme should always be included in a cook's herb garden. As soon as it has finished flowering, give the plant a trim to encourage new shoots.

THIS PAGE FROM LEFT Creeping thyme loves to grow in a hot, dry place where it can tumble over a wall or the edge of a container. Sage is an essential culinary herb, good in meat dishes.

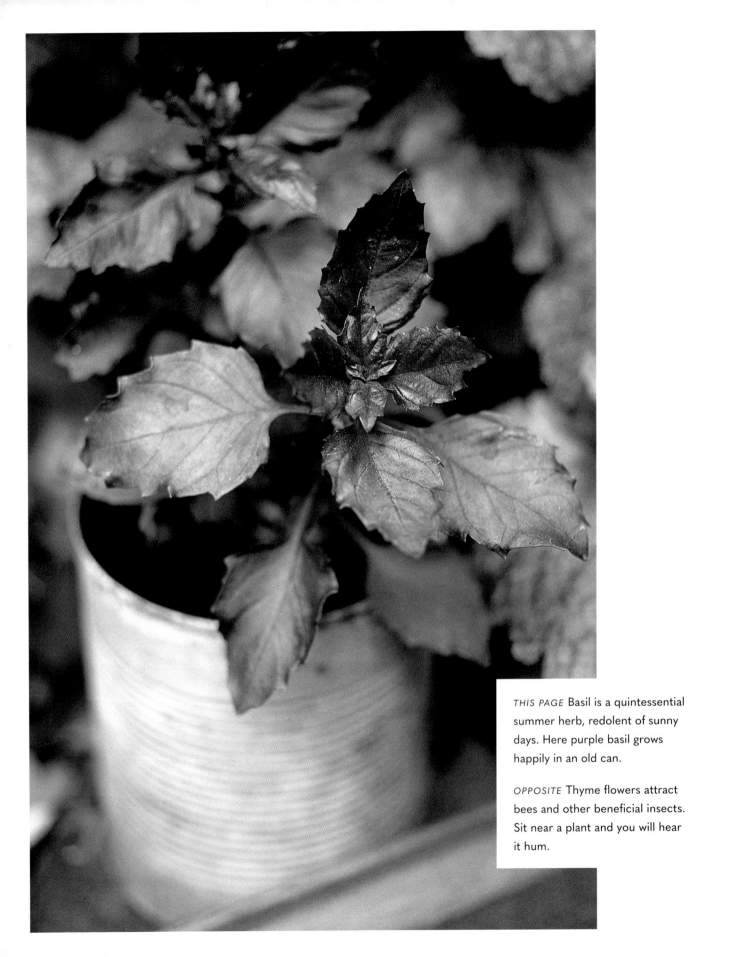

THIS PAGE Basil is a quintessential summer herb, redolent of sunny days. Here purple basil grows happily in an old can.

OPPOSITE Thyme flowers attract bees and other beneficial insects. Sit near a plant and you will hear it hum.

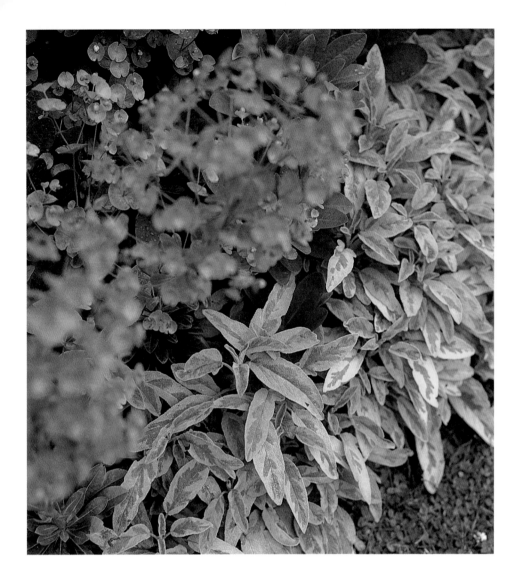

LEFT Sage comes in many varieties, some purely decorative and some palatable. *Salvia officinalis* is the culinary sage. This variegated form, *Salvia officinalis* 'Icterina', tastes as good as it looks. A tisane made from the leaves with added honey is good for sore throats. The petals of the flowers, removed from the leafy calyx, taste delicious.

Even in the tiniest herb garden, try and find space for the classic culinary herbs – parsley, sage, rosemary and thyme and a standard bay tree as well. In mild areas they can all be planted in the ground; elsewhere the less hardy plants, especially the rosemary and bay, may need to be planted in pots. Always use a soil-based compost with some added grit as this is much more suitable than compost containing peat or peat substitutes, which have a tendency to dry out in summer and conversely become waterlogged in winter.

Once you have grown lemon verbena you will never want to be without it. Brush past it and the air is filled with a delicate citrus fragrance. Its leaves can be used to make a wonderfully refreshing tisane and as a flavouring in fruit salads and cakes. Although not the easiest herb to grow, once you have found a position it likes it will survive outdoors in mild areas. A sun-baked corner at the base of a wall or a hot bank with poor, dry soil is what it likes best. This is another Mediterranean herb which hates to be wet in winter. Don't prune it until the first green shoots are showing in the spring. If grown in a pot it can be left to dry right out in the greenhouse – start watering moderately when spring is well advanced.

Many herbs are equally happy among flowers, so even if you haven't got an area dedicated to herbs you can still enjoy their aromatic qualities in the mindful garden. Plant prostrate thyme and rosemary in between paving slabs and you will release their fragrance as you walk along the path.

FRAGRANT HERBS

Aloysia triphylla (lemon verbena)

Anethum graveolens (dill)

Artemisia dracunculus (tarragon)

Borago officinalis (borage)

Carum carvi (caraway)

Chamaemelum nobile (chamomile)

Coriandrum sativum (coriander)

Foeniculum vulgare (fennel)

Laurus nobilis (bay)

Melissa officinalis (lemon balm)

Mentha (mint)

Ocimum basilicum (basil)

Origanum vulgare (marjoram)

Petroselinum (parsley)

Rosmarinus officinalis (rosemary)

Salvia officinalis (sage)

Satureja hortensis (summer savory)

Satureja montana (winter savory)

Thymus vulgaris (common thyme)

LEFT A perennial sweet pea twines its way through a rosemary bush. Rosemary is a highly aromatic herb, which bears its fragile blue flowers in the depths of winter. Frequent picking of the stems keeps the plant attractively bushy – left to its own devices it has a tendency to become leggy.

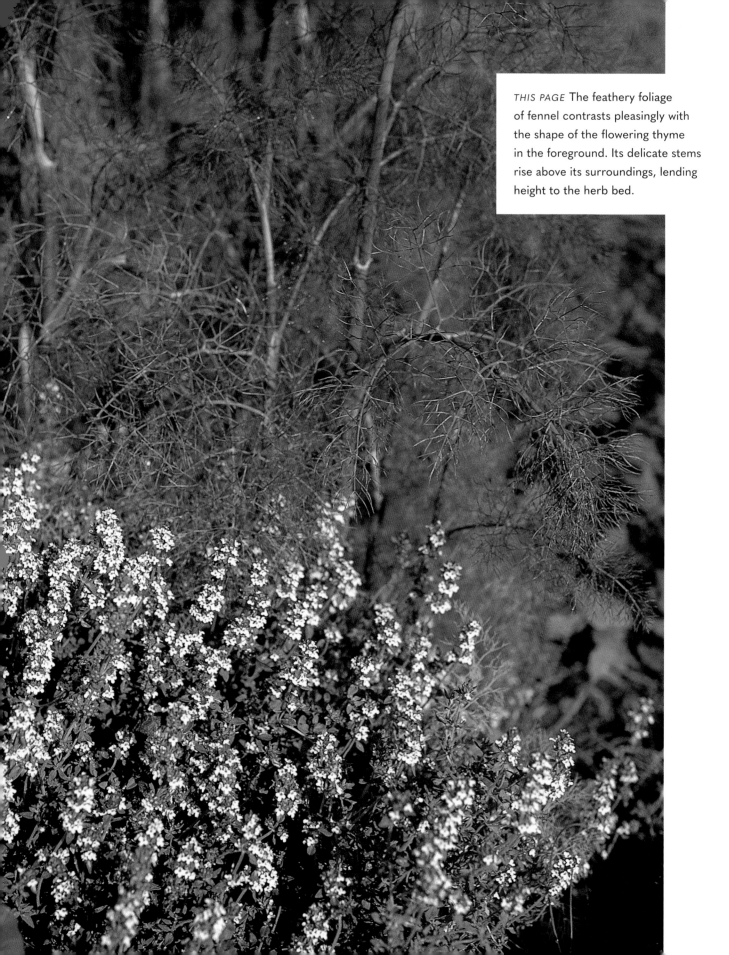

THIS PAGE The feathery foliage of fennel contrasts pleasingly with the shape of the flowering thyme in the foreground. Its delicate stems rise above its surroundings, lending height to the herb bed.

LEFT AND BELOW LEFT Mint is a refreshing and stimulating herb. Like sage, it comes in many varieties with different uses. While the woolly mint (left) can be used in the kitchen, many varieties, such as the variegated mint (below left), tend to be too perfumed to make enjoyable eating. Mint needs regular feeding and plenty of water to keep it growing well.

BELOW The non-flowering form of chamomile, 'Treneague', is ideal for lawns or seats. Taller growing chamomiles are cultivated for their flowers, which are used to make soothing tisanes and in other herbal remedies.

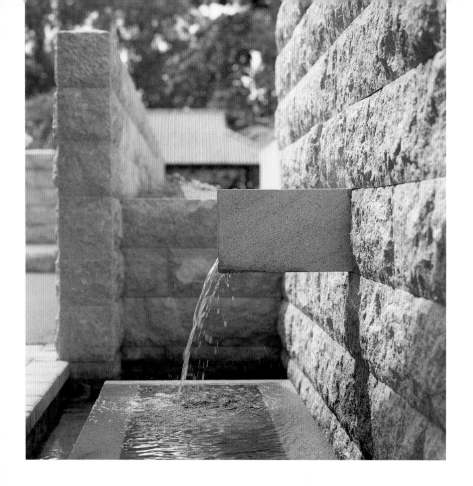

Cool water and rustling breezes

When we include a pond, a rill or a fountain in a peaceful garden it can make us more aware of the essential role of water in our lives. As we listen to its gentle splashing or gaze into a reflecting pool the water's presence is both reassuring and calming. Breezes ripple the surface of the water and rustle through the surrounding foliage.

For those of us who live in temperate climates where rain falls regularly and there is unlimited water flowing from our taps/faucets, it is easy to forget that water is a precious and often scarce commodity in many parts of the world. Historically, gardens could only exist where there was a reliable water source or where people had learnt to control and conserve their water. When the great gardens of the past were laid out, the control of water was frequently a central theme. The Persians piped water from distant mountains to make the desert bloom

in gardens where splashing fountains and gently flowing rills cooled the dry air. In England the aristocracy and wealthy landowners employed the likes of Capability Brown and Humphrey Repton to manipulate the landscape, damming rivers and employing many hundreds of workers over decades to dig ornamental lakes or create canals. In the gardens of Versailles, Villa d'Este and Chatsworth, water engineering reached its zenith with the creation of magnificent cascades and fountains. In these gardens water was more important than plants.

Today water is generally used on a more modest scale, even in public spaces. We all have the technology, most of us have sufficient water, and with nothing to prove it seems that many of us are content to restrict the water in our gardens to little more than an outside tap and a hosepipe or occasionally a concealed irrigation system. Expense is, understandably, an important consideration. Unless you are fortunate enough to have natural water running through your garden the addition of all but the most modest of ponds is going to involve major landscaping work. It is wise to consult an expert in these matters – a poorly designed water feature is worse than none at all, especially in a peaceful garden where all the elements should induce calm rather than irritation. Ponds that are too shallow cause the most problems. They have a tendency to turn green at the drop of a hat and rapidly fill with great curtains of algae encouraged by the warm, shallow water. Overhanging trees that drop their leaves will clog and pollute a pond – admittedly water can look very pretty in a shady spot, but such a pond will need netting in autumn and regular cleaning or it will degenerate into a smelly, stagnant bog.

OPPOSITE It isn't always necessary to re-landscape the garden in order to introduce water. A pond in a pot in a tiny garden conjures up the feeling of an inviting jungle pool, surrounded by rocky outcrops and lush vegetation.

ABOVE This dark, rectangular pond needs no embellishment. Its magnificent setting and its reflective qualities have a restrained perfection.

RIGHT A basement area outside a townhouse has been turned from a dingy, unattractive and unused space into a Japanese-inspired water garden. Underwater lighting has been set into the trough, so its calming presence is not overlooked in the evening. Materials are thoroughly urban and the planting is simple – bamboo, cotoneaster and an arum lily.

As with other design aspects of the mindful garden, the way water is used should be appropriate to the setting. A formal symmetrical garden requires a formal pond. Traditional materials that echo existing features are a safe bet, but providing the shape and the dimensions are right the use of contemporary materials can offer a more interesting solution. Simple, clean lines work best in a modern urban garden where the inclusion of falling or running water effectively masks the sound of traffic and freshens the air. In a country garden, a natural pond will blend into the landscape and look as if it has always been there. This type of pond takes time to establish and balance, but it is worth the effort and is ultimately a far more attractive solution than digging a hole and installing a preformed pond bought at a garden centre. For some unfathomable reason they are generally bright blue and strangely amoebic in shape, and it is hard to imagine any location where one would look appropriate.

Before embarking on any water feature it is essential to consider safety. If small children regularly use or visit

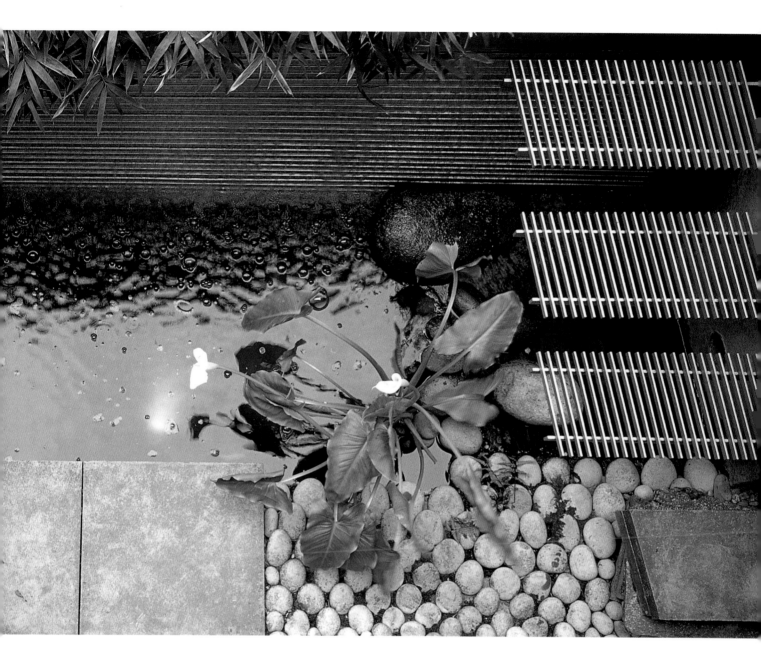

the garden, open water of any description is potentially dangerous. There will be little enjoyment if you have to be constantly on guard to avert tragedy. This does not mean though that water must be entirely excluded – a pebble fountain is a simple and safe way of introducing water into a small garden, or better still a water spout coming out of a wall and falling through a grating or onto stones at ground level is both safe and entertaining for children.

One of the great benefits of having water in the garden is the wildlife that it attracts – the dragonflies that

A great benefit of water in the garden is the wildlife it attracts – dragonflies that hover above the water with their iridescent wings, birds that drink and bathe in it, small mammals that visit, amphibians that take up residence and tiny water-boatmen that scoot over the surface.

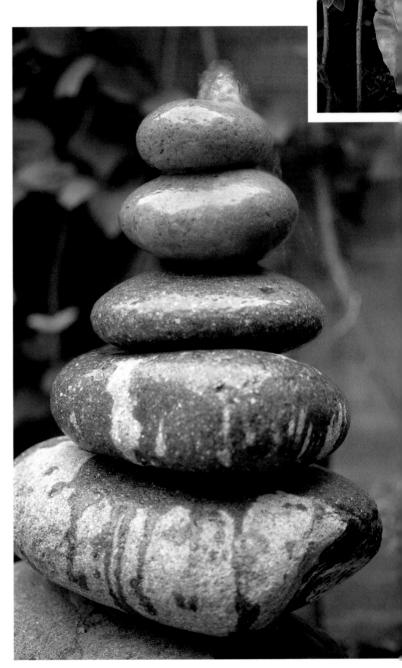

The way water is used should be appropriate to the setting. Simple, clean lines work best in a modern urban garden where the inclusion of falling or running water effectively masks the sound of traffic and freshens the air. In a country garden, a natural pond will blend in and look as if it has always been there.

hover above the water with their iridescent wings, the birds that drink and bathe in it, small mammals that visit, amphibians that take up residence and the tiny water-boatmen that scoot across the surface. If you need an excuse to linger in your mindful garden these creatures will provide it. Natural ponds provide the best environment with their shallow, gently sloping sides where marginal plants soften the edges and provide suitable wildlife habitats. A comfortable seat nearby will encourage you to sit and watch the life of the pond, and if the pond is large enough a rowing boat will allow a closer look.

Swimming pools can be a blot on the landscape, but a new development with its roots in Europe is set to change their appearance and their environmental impact in a dramatic way. Swimming ponds originated in Austria, where designers were looking for a way to make swimming pools wildlife friendly and less obtrusive. A central swimming pool is enclosed in an open tank, the top of which is just below water level, and this is surrounded by a gently sloping pond twice the size of the swimming area. Both pool and pond are lined with a dark, heavy-duty butyl liner. The pond is then lined with a deep layer of gravel and planted with a wide variety of aquatic and marginal plants, which act as oxygenators and water purifiers, doing away with the need for a filtration system. Once the swimming pond has settled down and plants are growing well there is little maintenance involved and wildlife and

OPPOSITE Water dribbles gently over these stones through a pipe inserted in a hole drilled through the stack. Even when the water isn't flowing, they have a sculptural quality.

LEFT A large ceramic bowl has been made into an eye-catching illuminated water feature.

humans co-exist happily in their different areas of the pond. A jetty leads from the bank to the central swimming pool where you can enjoy all the best aspects of swimming in natural water without scraping your knees on concealed rocks or getting entangled in weed.

Sympathetic planting around the margins of any pool or pond adds immeasurably to the atmosphere. Waterlilies love deep, still water and are suitable for both formal and natural ponds. Marginal plants grow best in the shallows, where their roots are in wet or boggy ground and their leaves and flowers are in the sun. As well as flowering plants such as arum lilies, candelabra primulas, astilbes, and Siberian irises there are foliage plants to sway in the breezes moving across the pond.

It is possible to create the illusion of flowing water in a garden with a still pond or even one with no water at all, using the sound of the wind rustling through leaves. In France, the wind blowing through the tall stands of poplar trees that punctuate the landscape sounds exactly like a rapidly flowing river. The giant grass *Arundo donax* and bamboos catch the breeze and emulate the sound of a babbling brook.

ABOVE Glass bricks were used to make this unusual water trough on a London roof terrace. Filled with pebbles, and with water splashing from above, there is not a plant in sight, but nonetheless there is a pleasant contrast of shapes and textures in the arrangement.

The sounds of plants are all around us once we have tuned in to them. I can stand in my own very sheltered garden with barely a zephyr ruffling my hair while the sound of the wind roars through the trees on the rim of the valley, wondering at the power of nature. Closer in, on a much smaller scale, I can hear the gentle popping of seedheads on a *Geranium palmatum* as it disperses its seeds, the rustle of dry leaves underfoot, and in the potager the gentle clatter of ripening runner-bean pods as they rattle against one another. These small, intimate sounds help focus the mind and sharpen the senses.

Some sounds are so slight that they are barely audible, but when combined with movement even they become apparent. This is particularly true with ornamental grasses – their gentle rustling could go entirely unnoticed, but the swaying of the leaves draws the eye and encourages closer examination. These small discoveries and pleasures contain within them the essential elements that can make any garden a mindful place and a personal sanctuary.

ABOVE LEFT Bamboo looks wonderful close to ponds or streams, where the rustling of the wind in their foliage adds atmosphere. Select the variety carefully, as many are rampant and their sharp shoots can pierce the strongest of pond liners.

RIGHT From left to right, the bamboos *Phyllostachys aurea* 'Holochrysa', *P. aurea* and *P. aurea* 'Koi' have contrasting stems and leaves. In a garden without water, the sound of the breeze rippling through their leaves creates the illusion of its presence.

OPPOSITE Ornamental grasses, like this *Stipa tenuissima* planted among pink astrantias, pick up every breeze and bring movement to the garden.

Business credits

Architects, designers and nurseries whose work and gardens are featured in this book:

Bedmar & Shi Designers Pte Ltd
12a Keong Saik Road
Singapore 089119
t. +65 22 77117
f. +65 22 77695
A Singapore-based firm
established in 1980,
specializing in residential
projects and also in interior
design, mainly for
restaurants and offices.

Jonathan Bell
11 Sinclair Gardens
London W14 0AU
t. 020 7371 3455
e. jb@jbell.demon.co.uk

Susan Berger & Helen Phillips
Town Garden Design
69 Kingsdown Parade
Bristol BS6 5UG
t./f. 0117 942 3843

Tania Compton
e. taniacompton@
madasafish.com

Cooper/Taggart Designs
t. +1 323 254 3048
e. coopertaggart@
earthlink.net

De Brinkhof Garden and Nursery
Dorpsstrat 46
6616 AJ Hernen
Holland
t. +31 487 531 486
Nursery and garden open
Friday and Saturday from
10am to 5pm, from April
until the end of September.
A small nursery specializing
in old-fashioned and unusual
varieties of hardy perennial.

Pierre & Sandrine Degrugillier
Le Mas de Flore
Lagnes 84800
France
t. +33 04 90 20 37 96
Antique and made-to-order
furniture.

Great Dixter Nurseries Northiam
Rye
East Sussex TN31 6PH
t. 01797 253107
f. 01797 252879
e. greatdixter@
compuserve.com

Isabelle C. Greene, F.A.S.L.A.
Isabelle Greene & Associates
2613 De la Vina Street
Santa Barbara
CA 93105
USA
t. +1 805 569 4045
e. icgreene@aol.com
Landscape architects
and land planners.

Gruga Park Botanic Gardens
Kulshammerweg 32
D 451
49 Essen
Germany

HDRA's Yalding Organic Gardens
Yalding Organic Gardens
Benover Road
Yalding, near Maidstone
Kent ME18 6EX
t. 01622 814650
www.hdra.org.uk
HDRA (Henry Doubleday
Research Association),
the Organic Association-
registered charity
researching and promoting
organic gardening, farming
and food. Open 10am to
5pm Wednesday to Sunday,
May to September,
weekends only during April
and October. Also open
Easter and all Bank Holiday
Mondays.

Judy M. Horton Garden Design
136 1/2 North Larchmont
Boulevard, Suite B
Los Angeles
CA 9004
USA
t. +1 323 462 1412
f. +1 323 462 8979
e. info@jmhgarden
design.com

Jan Howard
Room in the Garden
Oak Cottage
Furzen Lane
Ellens Green, Rudgwick
West Sussex RH12 3AR
t. 01403 823958
Manufacturers of elegant
designs in rusted iron.
Garden design services
by Jan Howard.
Catalogue available.

Ivan Hicks
t./f. 01963 210886
e. ivan@theedge88.fsnet.
co.uk
Garden and landscape
designer, land artist.

Iden Croft Herbs
Staplehurst
Kent
www.herbs-uk.com

Japanese Garden & Bonsai
Nursery
St Mawgan
Cornwall
t. 01637 860116

Johnson-Naylor Interior
Architecture
t. 020 7490 8885

Judy Kameon
Elysian Landscapes
724 Academy Road
Los Angeles
CA 90012
USA
t. +1 323 226 9588
f. +1 323 226 1191
www.plainair.com
Garden design and outdoor
furniture.

**La Bambouserie de
Prafrance**
301040 par Anduze
France
t. +33 68 61 70 47

Peter & Pam Lewis
Sticky Wicket
Buckland Newton
Dorchester
Dorset DT2 7BY
t./f. 01300 345476
Garden design, restoration
and management.

Dale Loth Architects
1 Cliff Road
London NW1 9AJ
t. 020 7485 4003
f. 020 7284 4490
e. mail@dalelotharchitects.
co.uk

Christina Oates
Secret Garden Designs
Fovant Hut
Fovant, nr. Salisbury
Wiltshire SP3 5LN
t. 01722 714756
www.secretgardendesigns.
co.uk
Garden designer Christina
Oates specializes in
imaginative and yet down-
to-earth consultancy visits
and concept plans.

**Sarah Raven's Cutting
Garden**
Perch Hill Farm
Brightling, Robertsbridge
East Sussex TN32 5HP
t. 01424 838181
f. 01424 838571
e. info@thecutting
garden.com
www.thecuttinggarden.com

Michael Reeves Interiors
33 Mossop Street
London SW3 2NB
t. 020 7225 2501
f. 020 7225 3060

**Suzanne Rheinstein
Associates**
817 North Hilldale Avenue
West Hollywood
CA 90069
USA
t. +1 323 931 340
and Hollyhock Hilldale
Address as above
Garden antiques and
accessories.
e. Hollyhockinc@aol.com

Rowden Gardens
Brentor
nr. Tavistock
Devon PL19 0NG
t./f. 01822 810275

Marc Schoellen
35 route de Colmar-Berg
L-7525 Mersch
Grand-Duché de
Luxembourg
t. +352 327 269
Garden historian and
amateur garden designer.

Roberto Silva
128 Hemingford Road
London N1 1DE
t. 020 7700 7484
e. landrob7@aol.com

Enrica Stabile
l'Utile e il Dilettevole
via della Spiga 46
20121 Milan
Italy
t. +39 02 76004820
www.utile-dilettevole.it
Antique furniture, garden
furniture, decorative objects,
soft furnishings, textiles.

Sally Storey
John Cullen Lighting
585 Kings Road
London SW6 2EH
t. 020 7371 5400
A wide range of practical
contemporary light fittings
as well as innovative made-
to-measure lighting design.

Derry Watkins
Special Plants
Greenways Lane
Cold Ashton
Chippenham
Wiltshire SN14 8LA
t. 01225 891686
e. specialplants@bigfoot.
com
www.specialplants.net
Opening hours 10.30am
to 4.30pm March to
September, other times
by arrangement; mail order
September to March only;
please send five second class
stamps for catalogue.

**Whitelaw Turkington
Landscape Architects**
t. 020 7820 0388

Stephen Woodhams
378 Brixton Road
London SW9 7AW
t. 020 7346 5656

Picture credits

All photography by Melanie Eclare unless otherwise stated.

Key: ph.=photographer; a=above; b=below; c= centre; l=left; r=right.

2 garden of interior designer Suzanne Rheinstein, designed by Judy M. Horton; 3 architect's house and garden in London designed by Dale Loth Architects; 4 l ph. Andrea Jones; 4 r ph. Pia Tryde; 5 c ph. Andrea Jones; 5 r ph. Andrea Jones; 6–7 Sticky Wicket wildlife garden near Dorchester, designed and created by Peter and Pam Lewis; 8–9 ph. Shirley Kemp/ Styling by Chris Myers; 10–11 a garden in south London designed by Roberto Silva; 12 l Connie Haydon's garden in Dorset; 12–13 Niall Manning and Alastair Morton's garden, Dundard, Fintry, Scotland G63 0EX; 14–15 the garden and nursery De Brinkhof of Riet Brinkhof and Joop Ven Den Berk; 16 & 17 l Carol Valentine's garden in California, designed by Isabelle Greene, F.A.S.L.A., a California landscape architect and planner; 17 r ph. Andrew Wood/'Melwani House' designed by Bedmar & Shi designers in Singapore; 18 Fiona Naylor and Peter Marlow's roof garden in London designed by Fiona Naylor and landscape architect Lindsey Whitelaw; 19 a house in Chelsea, lighting designed by Sally Storey; 20 - 21 a garden in London designed by Jonathan Bell; 22–23 the garden and nursery De Brinkhof of Riet Brinkhof and Joop Ven Den Berk; 24 & 25 Sticky Wicket wildlife garden near Dorchester, designed and created by Peter and Pam Lewis; 26–27 the garden of James Morris in Bristol designed by Sue Berger & Helen Philips; 28 Marc Schoellen's garden in Luxembourg called 'La Bergerie'; 29 Fiona Naylor and Peter Marlow's roof garden in London designed by Fiona Naylor and landscape architect Lindsey Whitelaw; 30 Jim Reynolds's garden 'Butterstream', Co. Meath, Ireland; 31 garden of interior designer Suzanne Rheinstein, designed by Judy M. Horton; 32 Connie Haydon's garden in Dorset; 33 & 34 l Jim Reynolds's garden 'Butterstream', Co. Meath, Ireland; 34–35 Niall Manning and Alastair Morton's garden, Dundard, Fintry, Scotland G63 0EX; 36 l ph Andrea Jones/Gruga Park Botanic Gardens; 36–37 the garden and nursery De Brinkhof of Riet Brinkhof and Joop Ven Den Berk; 38–39 Sticky Wicket wildlife garden near Dorchester, designed and created by Peter and Pam Lewis; 40–41 ph. Andrew Wood/'Melwani House' designed by Bedmar & Shi designers in Singapore; 42–45 Peter and SandraAitken-Quack's garden at Ham Cross Farm near Tisbury, designed by Tania Compton; 46 Fovant Hut Garden near Salisbury in Wiltshire was created by garden designer Christina Oates together with her husband Nigel and is open to the public; 47 l ph. Andrea Jones/ Japanese Garden and Bonsai Nursery; 47 r Jim Reynolds's garden 'Butterstream', Co. Meath, Ireland; 48 ph. Caroline Hughes/John and Joan Ward's garden in London; 49 ph. Andrea Jones/Great Dixter Nurseries; 50 Mr and Mrs James Hepworth's garden in Herefordshire; 51 the garden of James Morris in Bristol designed by Sue Berger & Helen Philips; 52–53 the garden and nursery De Brinkhof of Riet Brinkhof and Joop Ven Den Berk; 54 ph.Polly Wreford/Mary Foley's house in Connecticut; 55 Mr and Mrs James Hepworth's garden in Herefordshire; 56 the Farrell family, Woodnewton; 57 ph. Christopher Drake/Enrica Stabile's house, Le Thor, Provence; garden bench & cushions, l'Utile e il Dilettevole; 58 l a garden in London designed by Jonathan Bell; 58–59 Fiona Naylor and Peter Marlow's roof garden in London designed by Fiona Naylor and landscape architect Lindsey Whitelaw; 60 l Jim Reynolds's garden 'Butterstream', Co. Meath, Ireland; 60 r ph. Pia Tryde; 61 ph. Chris Tubbs; 62 ph. Caroline Hughes; 63 Mart Barlow's garden designed by Ivan Hicks; 64–65 a garden in south London designed by Robert Silva; 66 Mirabel Osler's garden in Ludlow, Shropshire; 67 & 68 al Hutton Wilkinson's garden designed by Tony Duquette; 68 ar Jan Howards garden in Sussex; 68 b Mirabel Osler's garden in Ludlow, Shropshire; 69 Mart Barlow's garden designed by Ivan Hicks; 70 ph. Caroline Hughes/Iden Croft Herbs; 71 Sticky Wicket wildlife garden near Dorchester, designed and created by Peter and Pam Lewis; 72 ph. Caroline Hughes/Iden Croft Herbs; 73 Sarah Raven's Cutting Garden in Brightling, designed by Sarah Raven; 74 Marc Schoellen's garden in Luxembourg called 'La Bergerie'; 75 Fovant Hut Garden near Salisbury in Wiltshire was created by garden designer Christina Oates together with her husband Nigel and is open to the public; 76–77 ph. Andrea Jones; 78 l ph. Francesca Yorke; 78 c ph. Caroline Hughes; 78 r ph. Pia Tryde; 79 Fovant Hut Garden near Salisbury in Wiltshire was created by garden designer Christina Oates together with her husband Nigel and is open to the public; 80 ph. Pia Tryde; 83 al ph. Andrea Jones; 83 br ph. Francesca Yorke; 84 ph. Andrea Jones; 85 ph. Caroline Arber/Rosemary Titterington at Iden Croft Herbs; 86 ar ph. Chris Tubbs; 86 bl ph. Pia Tryde; 86 br ph. Andrea Jones; 88 l ph. Andrea Jones/Rowden Gardens; 88 r ph.

Andrea Jones; 89 a Marc Schoellen's garden, 'La Berferie', in south London designed by Roberto Silva; 89 b ph. Pia Tryde; 90 l ph. Andrew Wood; 90 c & r Fiona Naylor and Peter Marlow's roof garden in London designed by Fiona Naylor & landscape architect Lindsey Whitelaw; 91 ph. Caroline Hughes/John and Joan Ward's garden in London; 92–93 ph. Catherine Gratwicke/Marja Walters – London, designed by Michael Reeves; 94 l a garden in London designed by Jonathan Bell; 94 ar ph. Andrew wood/'Melwani House' designed by Bedmar & Shi designers in Singapore; 94–95 b garden of interior designer Suzanne Rheinstein, designed by Judy M. Horton; 95 ar Fiona Naylor and Peter Marlow's roof garden in London designed by Fiona Naylor & landscape architect Lindsey Whitelaw; 96 Laura Cooper and Nick Taggart's Los Angeles garden, designed by Cooper/Taggart Designs; 97 ph. Andrea Jones/Stoners; 98 ph. Caroline Hughes/John and Joan Ward's garden in London; 99 al & c a garden in south London designed by Robert Silva; 99 b Mr & Mrs James Hepworth's garden in Herefordshire; 100 l ph. Chris Tubbs; 102–103 ph. Andrea Jones; 104 l Ph. Steve Painter; 105 r ph. Steve Painter; 106 ph. Andrea Jones; 107 ph. Christopher Drake/ Mr. & Mme. Degrugillier, Le Mas de Flore, Antiquite et Creation, Lagnes, Isle sur Sorgue, Provence; 108 Elspeth Thompson's garden in London; 109 l ph. Christopher Drake/antique lanterns – L'Utile e il Dilettevole; 109 r ph. Christopher Drake/Guido & Marilea Somare's house in Milan;110 Fiona Naylor and Peter Marlow's roof garden in London designed by Fiona Naylor & landscape architect Lindsey Whitelaw; 111 ph. Christopher Drake/Enrica Stabile's house in Provence; 112 - 113 ph. Christopher Drake/the late Giorgio & Irene Silvagni's house in Provence;

113 r ph. Tom Leighton; 114–115 the garden and nursery De Brinkhof of Riet Brinkhof & Joop Van Der Berk; 116 Laura Cooper and Nick Taggart's Los Angeles garden, designed by Cooper/Taggart Designs; 117 a Elspeth Thompson's garden in London; 117 b ph. Pia Tryde; 118–119 Derry Watkins's garden in Wiltshire designed by Derry Watkins and her husband, the architect Peter Clegg; 120–121 ph. Caroline Hughes/Iden Croft Herbs; 122–123 Sticky Wicket wildlife garden near Dorchester, designed and created by Peter & Pam Lewis; 124 ph. Stephen Robson; 125 ph. Caroline Hughes/Iden Croft Herbs; 126 ph. Stephen Robson; 127 ph. Caroline Hughes/Iden Croft Herbs; 128 ph. Caroline Hughes/HDRA's Yalding Organic Gardens, near Maidstone, Kent; 129 ph. Stephen Robson; 130 l ph. Francesca Yorke; 130 c ph. Pia Tryde; 130 r ph. Anne Hyde; 131 ph. Pia Tryde; 132–133 ph. Caroline Hughes/Iden Croft Herbs; 133 r ph. Caroline Arber; 134 –141 ph. Caroline Hughes; 142 ph. Andrew wood/'Melwani House' designed by Bedmar & Shi designers in Singapore; 143 ph. Andrea Jones/Japanese Garden & Bonsai Nursery; 144 ph. Jan Baldwin; 145 Niall Manning and Alastair Morton's garden, Dundard, Fintry, Scotland G63 0EX; 146–147 architect's house and garden in London designed by Dale Loth Architects; 148 l a house in Chelsea, lighting designed by Sally Storey; 148–149 a garden designed by Judy Kameon-Elysian Landscapes; 149 r Sarah Harrison & Jamie Hodder-Williams's roof terrace in London designed by Stephen Woodhams; 150 l ph. Andrea Jones; 150 r ph. Andrea Jones/La Bambouserie de Prafrance; 151 Sticky Wicket wildlife garden near Dorchester, designed and created by Peter and Pam Lewis; 153 ph. Andrea Jones; 154 ph. Andrea Jones; 160 ph. Pia Tryde.

Index

Page numbers in *italic* refer to illustrations

leaves
  colour 78, *88–9*
  shapes 25, 96
  texture 99–104
  variegated foliage 108
lemon balm 134, 139
lemon verbena 138, 139
Lewis, C. S. 70
Lewis, Peter and Pam *25*
light and shade 106–17
lighting *108–9*, *111*, *146–7*
lilies *126*, 130
  Madonna lily 123
  martagon lily 72
Lilium candidum 123
lily of the valley 123, 124
lime trees *51*
linear foliage 99, 100, 102
London 59, *64–5*, *149*
Lonicera 123
Los Angeles *116*
love-in-a-mist 88
low maintenance gardens *19*

M
Madonna lilies 123
Mahonia 124
  M. aquifolium 123
marjoram 85, 88, 134, 139
martagon lilies 72
Marvell, Andrew 78
masterwort 88
materials, texture 92–4
Matteuccia struthiopteris 88
Matthiola bicornis 120, 123
meadows 25, *71*, *122–3*
meditation 90, 92
Mediterranean plants 134, 138, 139
Melissa officinalis 130, 139
Mentha 139
mignonette 120, 123
miniature gardens 17
mint 134, 139, *141*
  variegated *141*
  woolly *141*
mirrors 66, 70
mock orange 123, 124
monastic gardens 47, 50, 90, 92
Monet, Claude 49
morning glory *80*, 88
mullein 104

N
narcissus 124
Nepeta 85, 88
Nigella 88
night lights 114, *117*
night-time gardens 113

O
Ocimum basilicum 139
olive trees 75
Omar Khayyam 75
opium poppy 88, 95
optical illusions 33, 66, 70
orange flowers 78
oregano 134
Oregon grape 123, 124
Origanum 85, 88
  O. vulgare 139
Osler, Mirabel 66

P
Paeonia lactiflora 123
palms 97
  sago palm *31*
Panicum virgatum 'Shenandoah'
  102
Papaver somniferum 88, 95
parsley 134, 138, 139
paths *12*, *13*, *24*, *25*, *36*, *72*, *89*,
  99
  balance *37*
  destinations 32–3
  perspective 33
  railway sleepers *96*
  scented plants *127*, *128*, *129*
  symmetry 30
  texture *99*
  through meadows *71*
pavilions 53–4
paving slabs, sitting areas 29
pebble fountains 147, *148*
pebbles 90, *90*, *94*, 95
Pelargonium tomentosum 95
peonies 123, 124
pergolas *48*, 114, *116*, 124, 127
Persian gardens 47, 50, 142
perspective, optical illusions 33
Petroselinum 139
Philadelphus coronarius 123
Phlox 124
  P. paniculata 123
phormiums 97
Phyllostachys aurea 150
  P. a. 'Holochrysa' 150
  P. a. 'Koi' 150
physic gardens 50
pink flowers 78, 82
planning, balanced gardens 36
plants
  fragrance 118–41
  ponds 149
  shapes 25, 96
  simplicity *22–3*, *24*, *25*
  special places 72–5
  textures 96, 99–104

ponds 29, *46*, *47*, *118–19*, 142,
  142, 144, 145–9, *145*
  floating candles 114
  jetties *46*
  reflections *28*, *31*, 53
  wildlife ponds *47*
poplar trees *149*
poppies
  California poppy 95
  opium poppy 88, 95
post and rail fences 16
potagers 15, 16, *32*
Primula vialii 83
primulas, candelabra *149*
privacy 18–19, 58, *59*, *60*
purple flowers 78, 82
pussy willow 95

Q
quaking grass *103*

R
railway sleepers *98*
reclamation yards 67
red flowers 78
reflections, ponds *28*, *31*, 53
relaxation 44–61
Repton, Humphrey *142*
Reseda odorata 120, 123
Rheum 99
rills 29, *29*, 50, 142
rocks, Zen gardens 90, 92
Romneya coulteri 95
roof gardens 18, 58, *59*
Rosa (rose) *42–3*, *51*, 75, 104,
  120–1, *125*, *126*, *127*, *128*,
  130
  R. 'Belle de Crécy' *127*
  R. gallica var. *officinalis* 123
  R. 'Louise Odier' *127*
  R. 'Madame Isaac Pereire' *127*
  R. 'Peace' *125*
  R. 'Roseraie de l'Haÿ' *127*
rosemary 72, *130*, 134, 138, *139*,
  139
roses *see Rosa* (rose)
Rosmarinus officinalis 139
rural gardens *94*
  wildflowers *25*

S
safety, water 146–7
sage 95, *100*, *130*, 134, *135*, 138,
  138, 139
sago palm *31*
Salix caprea 95
Salvia officinalis 95, 139
  S. officinalis 'Icterina' *138*

Santolina 85
Sarcococca 124
  S. humilis 123
Satureja hortensis 139
  S. montana 139
savory
  summer savory 139
  winter savory 139
scabious *25*
scented plants 72, 118–41
screens 18, 58
sculpture 33, *68*
sea holly 88
seating 29, 33, 60, *92–3*
  see also benches; chairs
The Secret Garden (Hodgson
  Burnett) 70
Sedum 95, 104
Senecio cineraria 102
senses, tranquillity for the 76–117
shady gardens 72, 106–17
shapes
  leaves 25, 96
  plant outlines 25, 96
  water features 29
shrubs, Zen gardens 90
Siberian irises *149*
Silva, Roberto *10–11*, *64–5*
simplicity 12–29
Sissinghurst, Kent 82
slugs 100
Smith, Joe *68*
snails 100
solar lighting 114
Somerset 70
sounds 149–50
special places 62–75
Stachys lanata 95, 104
stained-glass panels 70
star jasmine 123, 124
statues 33, *68*
stepping stones 90
steps *12*
Sticky Wicket, Dorset *25*, *38–9*
Stipa gigantea 102
  S. tenuifolia 95
  S. tenuissima 76–7, *151*
stocks, night-scented 120, 123
stone *33*, *94*, *94*, *99*
streams *143*
succulents *16*, *17*, *100*, *101*
summerhouses 53–4, *53*, 60,
  67, *114–15*
sunflowers *20*
sunny gardens 110, 124, 127
sweet peas 123, *124*, 130, 139
sweet rocket 88, 123
swimming pools *112–13*, *148–9*

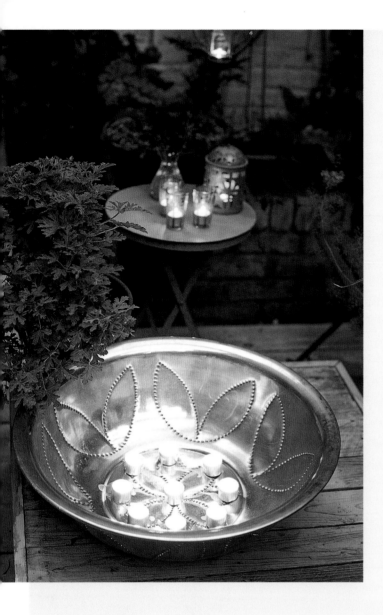